CONFESSIONS OF A
SCARY MOMMY

JILL SMOKLER

G

GALLERY BOOKS

NEW YORK LONDON TORONTO SYDNEY NEW DELHI

G

Gallery Books

A Division of Simon & Schuster, Inc.

1230 Avenue of the Americas

New York, NY 10020

Copyright © 2012 by Jill Smokler

First Gallery Books hardcover edition April 2012

GALLERY BOOKS and colophon are registered trademarks of Simon & Schuster, Inc.

For information about special discounts for bulk purchases, please contact Simon & Schuster Special Sales at 1-866-506-1949 or business@simonandschuster.com.

The Simon & Schuster Speakers Bureau can bring authors to your live event. For more information or to book an event contact the Simon & Schuster Speakers Bureau at 1-866-248-3049 or visit our website at www.simonspeakers.com.

Designed by Julie Schroeder
Scary Mommy logo designed by Jill Smokler
Illustrations by Amy Saidens

Manufactured in the United States of America

5 7 9 10 8 6

Library of Congress Cataloging-in-Publication Data is available.

ISBN 978-1-4516-7377-7
ISBN 978-1-4516-7378-4 (ebook)

For my children, Lily, Ben, and Evan.
Thank you for giving me the
greatest gift of all: motherhood.
I love you more than you can imagine.

CONTENTS

CONTENTS

FOREWORD

I am not a writer.

Sure, I wrote this book, but I am not an *actual* writer. At least, I don't think of myself that way.

I'm a graphic designer by trade, and I took some time off from work when my kids were babies. I knew I'd eventually have to go back to a salary to help pay the bills, but I was going to milk living in yoga pants and not showering until dinnertime for as long as I possibly could. There was nothing about wearing heels and lipstick to an office that I missed, but the slothfulness did come with a cost. While I certainly didn't miss the *work,* I missed having something—anything—to myself. Endless games of peekaboo and board books were not as fulfilling as I thought they would be; I felt like I was drowning in boredom and lame nursery rhymes. So, on a whim, I started a blog.

It seemed like as good a solution as any: I'd be able to keep a baby book of sorts for the kids—kind of a modern-day love letter—and it would give me something to focus on between laundry, diaper changes, and grocery shopping. Plus, it meant I wouldn't have to send those annoying picture-filled e-mails to friends and family. What did I have to lose? Nothing, it turned out, but I had no idea just how very much I would gain.

I wrote about my struggles to get the "perfect" photo of my children and my frustrations with the terrible twos. I shared cute little pictures and art projects and stories, but I never dreamed that anyone not closely connected to me would ever read them. But a few weeks in, something amazing happened: I got a comment from someone *other* than my mother or my best friend. Someone, from thousands of miles away, who had somehow found and related to me. I clicked on her name and found that she had a blog of her own, where she, too, shared her views on motherhood and parenting. They were different from mine but fascinating to read about. From there, I clicked around and found that there were hundreds, thousands of moms writing about their lives and views. It was a whole wide world I'd accidentally fallen into. And I was hooked.

As my site grew, so did the sense of community. Where I once felt alone in my feelings of exhaustion and imperfection, I suddenly had other moms from all around the world understanding and relating to me. Likewise, the honest thoughts about motherhood that had existed only in my head started creeping up on the blog. I began to consider my posts as facilitators for the larger discussion that took place in the comments. People added their own experiences and stories, and I laughed and cried and learned from them. We all have stories to tell, and I loved that people were using my space to open up with their own.

A few years after starting my site, I added an anonymous confessional, sensing that there was so much more my readers might say if they could do so without leaving a username or picture. The reaction was amazing. Some confessions were sad, some were pee-in-your-pants funny, and some were brutally honest, but they were *real*. You'll see confessions at the start of each chapter and that's where they're from. Real moms leaving real thoughts, without fearing judgment or negative reactions. I'm sure you'll be able to find reflections of yourself in at least a few of them. We're really not all that different from one another.

It's my hope that this book will act in much the same way my blog does. While you may not be able to comment on posts the way you would online, the book may inspire you to connect with people—to talk about some of the funny stuff and the hard stuff—in ways you might not have before. Open up with your friends about how hard it is to raise a girl. Admit to your neighbor how much you despise the pool. Use this book as a lifeline when you find yourself drowning in mommyhood.

To my Scary Mommy community members: Thank you. Thank you for showing me a side of me I never knew existed and for making a dream I never knew I had come true.

Chapter 1

BEING A
SCARY MOMMY

Mommy Confessions

• I confess that most days, I feel like I have no idea what I'm doing. Everyone thinks I have it all together—good wife, good mom, successful career—but I really don't. I'm ready to stop pretending to be perfect now.

• I tried for seven years to get pregnant and now that I'm a mother, I wonder whether it was all worth it.

• If I have to watch *Barney* one more time, I may have to stick a fork in my eye. Actually, then I'd get some attention. Maybe not such a bad idea.

• I sometimes try to get sick, just so I have an excuse to go to sleep at 6:00 p.m.

• I joined a gym just for the free day care. I drop the kids off and read magazines and blogs in the locker room.

• I pretend to be happy being a stay-at-home mom but sometimes I feel like I'm slowly dying. I cry every night in the shower. This isn't what I thought it would be.

• I kiss my young teenager good-bye in the morning as she leaves for school, rising above the hormone-fueled snarling and histrionics. Then I close the front door and flip her off, with both hands.

• I miss the career I gave up more than I miss my son when I go to the grocery store. But I always get to go back to him.

• Hidden in the pantry in a box labeled "flour" is top-of-the-line chocolate and a few joints. I rarely resort to it, but it's a comfort knowing it's there.

There are a million ironies in motherhood: The day you decide to change the sheets will inevitably be the night your child wets the bed. With a million toys in the house, your baby will without a doubt prefer to play with pots and pans from the kitchen cabinet than with any expensive learning game, and your kids will always fall asleep early for the sitter who gets paid by the hour to entertain them. It's unfair, uncool, and unjust, but, unfortunately, it's the way it is. Perhaps, though, the biggest irony out there is that despite never actually *being* alone (can you remember the last time you peed in peace?), as a mother you can feel totally isolated.

A few years ago, I was a stay-at-home mom to three kids, ranging in age from a newborn to a four-year-old. I was living in a new house, in a new town, among unfamiliar neighbors. It was lonely and overwhelming and I was bordering on miserable. A fellow mom from down the street stopped by our house to introduce herself and ask how my days were going. Half joking, I responded, "The baby is a bit of an asshole, but he'll grow out of it. We'll survive." The look on her face was enough to let me know not only that I had offended her, but that we would not be spending our afternoons commiserating together. She had three young kids, as well—was she not going slowly insane, too? Did she not long for an afternoon without kids wiping snot on her jeans and a baby spitting up constantly? Did she not lock herself in the bathroom, ignoring the whining on the other side of the door? Apparently not. Or she faked it a hell of a lot better than I was able to.

We like to paint motherhood as a picture-perfect experience, filled with idyllic children and beaming mothers. A perfect newborn peacefully resting on his mother's chest. A toddler taking tentative first steps into the loving arms of his mother, who is smiling proudly and wiping tears of joy from her cheeks. A mother's long, blond hair trailing in the wind as she holds hands with and runs alongside her beautiful, impeccably dressed children. A mother and daughter sipping tea and painting each other's nails, telling each other their deepest secrets and dreams. A mother leading Girl Scout troops and chairing PTA events and fluffing her daughter's prom dress before her nervous date knocks on the front door.

Those moments of motherhood are indeed miraculous and joyful; they can also be few and far between.

What if that baby never latches properly and breast-feeding becomes a nightmare that results in both baby and mother sobbing for hours on end? What if instead of happily reading together with her child for hours, the mother of a tough toddler wonders, just for an instant, whether there is something more to life than puzzles and ABCs? What if a mother, once her teenage child leaves the door, breathes a sigh of relief that the drama is temporarily on hold and drinks a glass of wine alone in the bathtub?

Do these things make motherhood any less perfect?

Of course not: they make motherhood *real*.

Motherhood isn't a chain of wondrous little moments strung together in one perfectly orchestrated slide show. It's dirty and scary and beautiful and hard and miraculous and exhausting and thankless and joyful and frustrating all at once. It's *everything*. Anyone who claims that motherhood is only the good stuff is simply in denial (or she's on some serious drugs). Admitting that this job isn't always easy doesn't make somebody a bad mother. At least, it shouldn't.

We're all on this ride together. We are not the first ones to ever accidentally tell our children to shut up, or wonder—just for a moment—what it would be like if we'd never had children. We aren't the first mothers to feel overwhelmed and challenged and not entirely fulfilled by motherhood. And we certainly won't be the last.

Nothing can be lost by admitting our weaknesses and imperfections to one another. In fact, quite the opposite is true. We will be better mothers, better wives, and better women if we are able to finally drop the act and get real. Who are we pretending for, anyway? It is my hope that no other mother feels as alone as I felt those first few months of motherhood. There are millions of us mothers, all feeling the same way, all across the globe. All we need to do is find one another.

Scary Mommies of the world, unite!

The Scary Mommy MANIFESTO

Please solemnly recite the following before proceeding:

★ I shall maintain a sense of humor about all things motherhood, for without it, I recognize that I may end up institutionalized. Or, at the very least, completely miserable.

★ I shall not judge the mother in the grocery store who, upon entering, hits the candy aisle and doles out M&M's to her screaming toddler. It is simply a survival mechanism.

★ I shall not compete with the mother who effortlessly bakes from scratch, purees her own baby food, or fashions breathtaking costumes from tissue paper. Motherhood is not a competition. The only ones who lose are the ones who race the fastest.

★ I shall shoot the parents of the screaming newborn on the airplane looks of compassion rather than resentment. I am fortunate to be able to ditch the kid upon landing. They, however, are not.

★ I shall never ask any woman whether she is, in fact, expecting. *Ever.*

★ I shall not question the mother who is wearing the same yoga pants, flip-flops, and T-shirt she wore to school pickup the day before. She has good reason.

★ I shall never claim to know everything about children other than my own (who still remain a mystery to me).

★ I shall hold the new babies belonging to friends and family, so they may shower and nap, which is all any new mother really wants.

★ I shall strive to pass down a healthy body image to my daughter. She deserves a mother who loves and respects herself; stretch marks, dimples, cellulite, and all.

★ I shall not preach the benefits of breast-feeding or circumcision or homeschooling or organic food or co-sleeping or crying it out to a fellow mother who has not asked my opinion. It's none of my damn business.

★ I shall try my hardest to never say never, for I just may end up with a loud mouthed, bikini-clad, water gun–shooting toddler of my very own.

★ I shall remember that no mother is perfect and that my children will thrive because of, and sometimes even in spite of, me.

Chapter 2

THIS IS SUPPOSED TO
BE BEAUTIFUL?

Mommy Confessions

• I look at my pregnant stomach and cringe. I'm supposed to feel all glowing and wonderful, but I just feel fat and ugly.

• Is it normal to be this horny during pregnancy? I swear, I'm about to jump my obese fifty-seven-year-old plumber. What the hell?

• That three-second orgasm was SO not worth this nine-month hell.

• I pee when I cough, I fart when I sneeze, and I'm sure I'll crap on the delivery table.

• My husband is convinced he's going to bang the baby's head during sex. Honey, I've seen your thing and NO WAY can it reach that far. Not even close.

• My pregnancy has been blissfully easy, but I pretend to be crippled with exhaustion just so I can be alone. Otherwise, I might kill my husband.

• I've taken a three-hour nap every day of my pregnancy. I could stay pregnant forever and be happy.

• I ate a jar of Nutella a month while pregnant. Okay, a jar a week. Okay, okay, a day. A jar of Nutella a day. I've never admitted that before.

• My pregnant boobs are like crazy, porn-star boobs. I think I might need to become a surrogate just to keep tits like this.

• I spent every day pissed off at this unborn baby for making me so ill. He's not even born and I'm a terrible mother.

• I'm afraid I won't be able to love this new baby as much as my daughter. The fear consumes me.

• If pregnancy is any reflection on what kind of mother I'll be, I may as well give this kid up for adoption.

• I'm eating for three. Problem is, I'm only expecting one and she's the size of a pea right now.

• Up at 3:00 a.m. waxing my legs and bikini area, manicure/pedicure, exfoliating, the works. Not for a hot date—I've got an OB appointment tomorrow. It's the most action I'll see all month.

My firstborn child was—how do I say this eloquently?— a very pleasant surprise! No, that's not true. She was a complete and utter shock. A hysteria-inducing, this-cannot-be-happening-to-me, why-did-I-not-triple-up-on-the-birth-control shock that rocked my selfish, skinny life to the very core. Just so we're clear.

Back in 2003, I was working in store design for my favorite company. My simple life consisted of shopping, eating out with my husband, drinking with friends, and shopping some more. Did I mention shopping? Because it was the biggest part of my life. My job, which involved decorating a beautiful store with things I could buy myself at a steep discount, was the perfect fit for a self-absorbed girl like me.

My job required me to arrive early so I could unpack and arrange the merchandise that had arrived the previous day on the sales floor. One particular morning in May at about five o'clock, I sat on an overpriced shag carpet with my coworkers, tearing into the big cardboard boxes that had arrived from far overseas. Shiny amethyst earrings! Embellished scarves! Miniature teacups! Everything was so totally cute and absolutely worth spending my entire paycheck on. What else was money for, anyway? Certainly not for saving or investing in anything. Who needed that?!

After a while, I got to a box containing nothing but cookbooks. Beautiful cookbooks that normally made my mouth water and dream of dining on sea bass and grilled vegetables and whatever other beautiful dishes were spread across the colorful pages. But, as I pulled the first one out and glanced at the cover, a funny thing happened. Actually, it wasn't so funny at all. The mere sight of a plate of roasted scallops sent me running into the bathroom for dear life. Scallops, normally one of my favorite foods, were suddenly unbelievably repulsive. So repulsive that I could barely control myself, and before I knew it, the entire contents of my stomach covered the stockroom bathroom. That was odd, I thought. Maybe I had some bad Honey Nut Cheerios for breakfast? Yes, that must have been it. *Of course.*

The rest of the day went similarly. Suddenly, I couldn't look at food without needing to upchuck. A coworker heated up her lunch in the communal microwave and the grotesque smell infuriated me. Wasn't the stench of homemade ravioli revolting to anyone else? The tomato sauce? The cheese? The faint scent of garlic and onion? So rude of her to heat up her food like that and torture the rest of us! It was gag-worthy, wasn't it? Except, it wasn't. Not to anyone else but me.

"You're totally pregnant," my assistant observed confidently when I returned from my seventh trip to the ladies' room. "Pregnant? Me? No way. I'm just . . . off today," I responded in a huff. Certainly, that was it . . . I *couldn't* be pregnant. We lived in a third-floor walk-up downtown, I'd had three vodka tonics last weekend, I was rocking the supershort denim skirts, I didn't even *like* kids, for crying out loud. It was simply *not* a possibility. Maybe there was a stomach bug going around—maybe I'd even drop a few pounds in the process! Now, *that* I could deal with. But pregnant? Nope. Not me.

On the way home, I stopped at the drugstore to pick up some Pepto-Bismol and a trashy magazine. I happened to pass the family-planning aisle, where the pregnancy tests stared back at me from their orderly little shelves. *Of course* it would be negative, and I would relish in saying "I told you so" tomorrow at work, but what the hell? The ten bucks seemed worth the investment if for no other reason than to prove my coworkers wrong. I'd certainly spent money on more frivolous things in my lifetime. Into my cart the little test flew.

At my apartment, I ripped open the package and followed

the directions diligently. Prepared to wait awhile in the bathroom, I thumbed through my hot-off-the-press *People* magazine to catch up on the latest Jen and Brad gossip: Were they expecting? Was he cheating? Was *she* cheating? When was the last time he shaved that beard? Her hair was a little too blond, but not altogether bad. Would mine look good like that? It might look good on me . . .

These were my priorities until I saw two blue lines appear on the test. Suddenly, I had much bigger things to worry about. Brad who?

I frantically dialed my husband at work. "Jeff," I stammered. "Um. I just took a pregnancy test . . . and it was positive." Dead silence followed on the other end. Hellooo? "I'm coming home," he whispered, and hung up the phone. In record time, armed with overflowing drugstore bags, he arrived at the door. Five minutes later, we had a buffet of pregnancy tests decorating the bathroom sink. They varied in color, size, and brand, but all had one thing in common and there was no doubt about it. Life as we knew it was over.

I suppose it shouldn't have been all that much of a shock as I *had* gone off the pill a few months ago. But that wasn't to get *pregnant*! Hell, no. It was just to get my skin cleared up and give my body a break before going on a *different* pill. My gynecologist's reminder to make sure to practice backup birth control floated around my head in an imaginary cartoon bubble.

Once the immediate shock and denial wore off, I tried to look on the bright side: We *were* a happily married couple. It was totally acceptable for happily married couples to reproduce. I had, after all, handpicked this man to spend the rest of my life with. If I were going to have a child with anyone, *he* was the one

I wanted to do it with. Maybe it really was meant to be, in some bizarre, cosmic way that I couldn't yet grasp. Perhaps this pregnancy thing wasn't all that bad.

And then I threw up.

The "morning" sickness was just the beginning. It amazed me that a creature, barely the size of a peanut, could be wreaking such havoc on my body. I was exhausted, like I had never known exhaustion before. But, as fatigued as I was, I couldn't actually sleep. Such an unfair predicament. My skin was breaking out like I was an oily teenager again. My back ached. My hair curled funny. My nails split. I was a mess. This bullshit was beautiful? Please tell me exactly what is beautiful about any of it, because I seemed to have missed that part.

As if I didn't feel shitty enough, my body and business suddenly seemed to be part of the public domain. I wasn't even a mother yet, and I was being judged for decisions I had yet to make. It was the motherhood rat race, and I was an unintentional contender. Strangers would stop me in restaurant bathrooms and ask whether I planned on breast-feeding. How on earth was that information relevant to them in the least? Old ladies questioned my choice of lunch meat, when they hadn't been pregnant in the last fifty years. Friends gave me unsolicited advice on cloth diapers and breast pumps, when I barely knew what either was. Don't even get me started on sleep training and circumcision. Once you're carrying a child, suddenly the world has an opinion on each and every choice you make, despite the fact that they have less than nothing to do with your decisions or the outcome. How this is socially acceptable is beyond me, especially with all of the hormones pregnant women are high on. Hasn't some nine-months-pregnant woman on the edge scared away the nosy busy bees yet? If I ever get pregnant again, I vow to be that person. For *you*.

And then there was my husband. My sweet, wonderful, and loving soul mate of a man, who, I successfully convinced myself, might actually be able to give me the only child on earth I'd ever be able to tolerate. Our very best qualities would merge and result in a baby who would change my view on all young people across the land. There must have been something primal about my attraction to him. It was all meant to be, I thought.

But, suddenly, this man I'd picked transformed into the most irritating creature I'd ever laid eyes on. What the hell had I done? The humor I'd previously found laugh-out-loud funny was now nothing but annoying. His snoring kept me up at night. The smell of his skin made me sick. He had the audacity to tell me that pregnant women looked sexy in heels—did he have to waddle around with bunions and balance issues? He simply could do no right. He and everyone else in the universe.

The whole experience made me wonder: Who *are* these women who blissfully glide through pregnancy? I have friends who claim to have enjoyed every moment of their trips to newbornville. They had precious little basketball tummies and glowing, dewy skin. They dressed in maternity bikinis and trotted around the swimming pool, putting us veiny, stretch mark–covered messes to shame. Had they not been with child, I'm quite sure I would have kicked them in the gut. While in heels.

And what about those freaks of nature who somehow get through all nine months never actually knowing that they're expecting? I mean, who *are* they?! With my subsequent pregnancies, I swear I knew the minute we conceived. The wave of nausea, the constipation, the slight change in everything about me . . . I can't imagine going a few weeks without knowing, never mind months on end. I will be eternally jealous of women like that. I can only pray that they end up with colicky babies. It only seems fair.

For a brief period of time, when I was around seven months pregnant or so, I got a taste of how the other half lives. For a few weeks, I wasn't a raging bitch from hell. I'd stopped throwing up constantly and was actually enjoying eating again. So much so that I impressively managed to pack on nearly thirty pounds by that point. It really was a medical marvel considering my inability to digest anything for the first few months. I finally looked pregnant—not just pudgy—and gained some energy back as well. Things were looking up. And then I hit the ninth month.

I wish the government could bottle the discomfort that accompanies this point in pregnancy—the bloating and the aches and pains and the baby's kicks. I think if they were able to inflict all of this on even the strongest of men, those men would cave under pressure. It would be the best torture method ever. If I thought the beginning was bad, I was sorely mistaken. The end? Pure misery.

When I was thirty-nine weeks pregnant, I woke up in the middle of the night feeling just a little bit off. I was restless and sweaty and started having stomach cramps. Not "baby is coming" stomach cramps but "I really need to take a big dump" stomach cramps. That much I was sure of. I called my mom to see what she suggested I take: Pepto? Colax? A Coke? It definitely didn't *feel* like labor, I reported (of course I had absolutely no idea what the hell labor was supposed to actually feel like), but I wanted to feel better. It was highly unpleasant. "Honey," she calmly explained, "that's exactly what labor feels like. This is it."

And that was my introduction to motherhood. Who knew that this totally new experience would echo something with which I was so well acquainted. It felt eerily familiar, highly uncomfortable, and not at all like I expected. In a word, it felt like shit.

And it was only just beginning.

Chapter 3

YES, YOU'LL SHIT ON THE DELIVERY TABLE

Mommy Confessions

• I'd rather have just about anyone other than my husband as my birth coach. Love him, but he's totally going to steal my thunder.

• My newborn looks like an alien. Am I supposed to find her cute?

• I resent my children for the marks they left on my body. My boobs are deflated, my stomach a mess, and I'm covered in stretch marks. Thanks, kids.

• To the new mom who left the hospital looking like a million bucks: I hate you.

• My son came out looking just like my ex-boyfriend. My first thought upon seeing him: Asshole.

• I had an elective c-section. I've never told a soul that it wasn't medically necessary; I just didn't want my body going through labor.

• I can't wait for delivery. That stay in the hospital is going to be as much of a vacation as I'll get this whole year.

• I am terrified of dying on the delivery table. The fear consumes me.

• Childbirth is the single most disgusting experience I've ever had in my life.

• Since childbirth, my husband is unable to satisfy me. Think I need to trade in his dick for a bigger model.

• Once a woman asked me whether I planned to breast-feed my baby, so I asked her whether she shaved her vagina. Oh, I'm sorry, you don't like personal, none-of-your-business questions?

• Since having a baby, all I can imagine during sex is the image I saw in the mirror. I will never look at my vajayjay the same way again.

• Childbirth was the highlight of my motherhood career. My kids are eight, ten, and twelve.

• Even my vagina has stretch marks.

Back when I was six months pregnant or so, Jeff and I signed up for childbirth classes at the local hospital where I was scheduled to deliver. We sat in the back row of a lecture room and listened as the aging nurse-practitioner dryly told us exactly what to expect from this "miraculous" event we were about to experience. Never one to be a good student, I found myself doodling potential baby names mindlessly to pass the time so that Jeff and I could go get pizza down the street. Yum, pizza . . .

Before long, the two of us were playing hangman and tic-tac-toe while the other expectant parents studiously took notes. If class was any indication of future parenting success, we'd already failed big-time. Suffice to say, we didn't get much out of that first lecture. We never went back for the rest of the sessions and figured we'd just wing it—childbirth couldn't be that complicated, right? Women had been doing it forever without lessons like these; surely it must come naturally. Like conception. We'd be fine.

As my due date quickly approached, I casually remarked to a friend that we'd never finished our prenatal classes. Instead of laughing it off, she was outraged: How would we know what to do when the time came? How would we advocate for ourselves? What was our birth plan? What were our choice labor positions? How did I feel about pain medication? What about fetal monitoring? Labor augmentation? Each word out of her mouth grated on my nerves more than the last. Holy shit, woman. My birth plan was to have a freaking baby! I'd huff and I'd puff and I'd push that baby right out . . . wasn't *that* enough of a plan? It wasn't, she convinced me. At the very least, it was my job to be educated. If not for myself, for my child. Already, the mother-guilt was commencing.

This friend, who is no longer such a friend, did succeed in making me nervous enough to actually thumb through a pregnancy book. Maybe she was right—it might not be the worst idea ever to have *some* idea of what to expect from this whole thing. Better to be prepared, I supposed. What did I have to lose?

The first chapters of my chosen book were a breeze, but the more I read on, the more horrified I became: First came the mucus plug. There was actually a plug keeping things staying put up there? Literally, a plug made of mucus? I could hardly blow my nose without gagging. Then I got to the chapter on episiotomies and vaginal tearing. I'd naively assumed that my body was made to open up like a floodgate and close back up, effortlessly. Not always, I found. I could actually tear my vagina open? And need stitches to sew me back together again? My lady parts ached just reading the words. But the worst part of the book to me was the small warning at the end. It was almost an afterthought, as if it didn't deserve much attention. Beware, it read, that when pushing the baby out, it is not uncommon for "other substances" to be pushed out as well.

OMG.

Seriously? "Other substances"?! I couldn't even pee with the door open! For the first five years of our relationship, Jeff was convinced that my body was unable to produce gas (a lot of "silent but deadlies" and blaming of the innocent dog, in case you were wondering). The thought of actually pooping in front of him along with a roomful of people was simply too much for me to process. Couldn't I just sign up for an elective c-section? I'd rather have major surgery than be humiliated like that. Perhaps I wasn't up for this whole thing after all.

A few weeks later, I had no choice. I found myself pacing the halls of the hospital, attempting to get my water to break "naturally." Always one for a fun scene, I was rather looking forward to a big flood of water as I stood up after dinner or waddled through the mall during the busy lunch hour. No such luck, and my water had to be broken manually (which, for the record, is not nearly as fun as it sounds). The start of my labor was *so* not how I imagined my Hollywood delivery would be. I should have known better by then. There ain't nothing glamorous about childbirth.

The rest of my labor went similarly. You know how in the movies and on TV, it's three pushes and the baby comes out? In my dreams. With all of my deliveries, it was hours of resting and monitoring and poking and prodding. I was actually bored. When it was finally time to push, I was *ready*. I was in the zone. Bring it on! I was woman, hear me roar!

But I didn't. Roar, I mean. I'd opted for the drugs early on so I wouldn't be in pain, and I wasn't. None at all. It was the best decision I could have made. Seriously, highly recommend, five stars, two thumbs up. What I *do* regret, however, was letting Jeff know exactly how little pain I was in. Because of my honesty (always my downfall, dammit) I am completely unable to pull the birth trump card. When he's whining about a cold, my "Well, I bore children and complained less!" isn't nearly as effective as it could have been. It sucks. My advice to you, future mothers: Get the drugs, but fake the pain. It's a win-win.

When I finally grunted Lily out, along did come a little something else, but it wasn't even a blip on the radar at that moment. Actually, being able to piss and shit openly was oddly liberating. Kind of relaxing, even. Plus, I had a far more important thing to concentrate on. Something that, eight years later, still infuriates me. From the moment my daughter came out, one thing was clear: She didn't resemble me in the least. She did, however, look eerily like her other DNA contributor, whom we shall now refer to as "the prick who trumped my genes."

I mean, seriously, what the hell? I carried this child for *nine months*. She bruised my insides and caused my feet to grow and hips to spread and made a road map of my stomach. I had to get rid of my favorite heels for her! And my skinny jeans! What did *he* do? He made a deposit and went on his merry way, that's what. I knew one thing for sure: the gene pool was bullshit. And I was pissed.

Also bullshit? That moment immediately after birth that I'd been waiting for. I'd watched enough soaps and movies to know what those precious moments would be like: The nurse would place my hollering baby on me and she would latch onto my breast and I would instantly feel like a mother. The clouds would open and light would shine in and we would be surrounded by rainbows and butterflies and happiness.

Or not.

I wanted my money back.

Instead of a perfect pink baby, I was given a slimy, nasty-looking thing whose head looked like it belonged in a dated *Saturday Night Live* sketch. She was gooey and blotchy and looked like she'd just been in a major fistfight. Unfortunately, she also looked like she'd lost. Big-time. Fortunately, she cleaned up well. (Thank God.)

But even all tidied up, I didn't feel the immediate outpouring of love that I was expecting. I felt relief that my months of puking up prenatal vitamins hadn't resulted in two heads and twelve fingers. I felt grateful that she didn't need to be carted off to the NICU or have a barrage of tests. I felt ecstatic to no longer be pregnant. And I certainly felt protective of her tiny little body. But love? How do you feel immense love for someone you don't even know?

I wanted to get to know her, though, and I wanted to do that at home. I was ready for us to begin our lives together. I missed my dog and I wanted to sleep in my own bed. Plus, I really needed a good shower and the hospital didn't have all of my yummy shampoos and body washes. Home sweet home. I could almost taste it.

In retrospect, I have no idea what the hell I was thinking. With my subsequent children, I was smart enough to know that the hospital is a pleasure cruise compared to what I had waiting for me at home. With my last, I practically had to be escorted out in handcuffs. Seriously, if I'd had them, I would have cuffed myself to the bed.

At the hospital, you have 24/7 nursing care. You have room service (it may not be five-star quality, but at least you don't have to cook). You have power over the remote control. You have a bed to yourself. You have a private bathroom. And, if you're really smart, you'll send the baby to the nursery and actually sleep. It's the most relaxed you'll have been in months. And the most relaxed you will be for a long, long time to come. Oh, one of the many things you just can't appreciate with a firstborn child. Really, it's reason enough to try for another one.

There's nothing like that trip home, though, whether it's your first or (God help you) your tenth. You have a new baby, a fresh outlook, and the world is your oyster.

Until you walk through your front door.

Chapter 4

ARE THEY REALLY LETTING ME TAKE THIS THING HOME?

Mommy Confessions

• After pouring my coffee, I realized we were out of milk. I used breast milk instead. Not bad.

• I wonder whether the other people hate me for having such good-looking babies . . . everyone should just quit trying at this point. It's been done.

• My baby's vibrating bouncy seat broke yesterday, so now my "top of the drawer" toy is wrapped in a receiving blanket and tucked into the side of the car seat. Desperate times call for desperate measures.

• I'll never understand baby gas . . . or how it can keep them up screaming all night. When else in life does this ever happen?

• Neurotic first-time moms annoy the shit out of me.

• I cried the first time my son cried inconsolably because I felt like a failure and wondered why God would ever let me be a mom.

• Newborns are UGLY. Yes, even mine.

• I am SO thankful that I ended up with an undeniably cute baby.

• When I married my husband he could do no wrong . . . when we started having babies he could do no right.

• Everyone loves the smell of new babies, but I thought mine stunk!

• "Sleep when the baby sleeps" is the most irritating, useless thing ever said to a new mother. I'm going to slap the next woman who says it. Because I know she didn't sleep when the baby slept. No one does.

• If babies were sleeping through the night at ten months old, I'd probably have seven more.

• I like my children best when they are newborns. I like them less every year after.

• Women everywhere should shield their babies' chubby thighs from my view . . . I refuse to keep my hands to myself.

• My baby is the only baby in the world who doesn't look like an ugly bald old man to me.

The first weekend that we got back from our honeymoon, Jeff and I ran out as fast as we could and bought a puppy. I remember driving out to the breeder's house several hours away and observing the precious little litter all playing together happily in the backyard, cute as could possibly be. After we picked out our tiny orange fur ball, the breeder sat down with us and drilled us on every detail of our lives: What was our house like? How many floors did it have? How flexible was our schedule? Did we travel on weekends? Had we explored puppy training? Did we have other dogs? Children? A housebreaking plan? Good Lord, this is intense, we communicated through eye rolls and side glances. But we diligently answered all of her questions and more. At the end of the interrogation, we were rewarded with an adorable eight-week-old golden retriever, who we immediately named Penelope. The woman handed us the papers, along with a list of puppy resources and veterinarians. Off we went, our new little family, confident that we had everything we needed to raise a happy and healthy dog.

Leaving the hospital with Lily was an entirely different experience. I was shocked that the nurses didn't ask us a single time whether we knew how to feed her or change her or soothe her in the middle of the night. They didn't want to inspect our home to see whether it was baby-ready or do a thorough background check on either one of us. They didn't ask for college transcripts or even whether we were CPR certified—we could have been serial killers and they wouldn't have known or cared. At the end of my two-day stay, they simply plopped me in a wheelchair and pushed me out the front door. Jeff and I looked at each other incredulously—*that* was it? Why was bringing home a puppy a thousand times more complicated? Where was my take-home fact sheet to refer to in the wee hours of the night when we had no idea what the hell to do? Where was my money-back guarantee? I'd never felt so unprepared for anything in my life.

It must have been obvious to the world that I had no clue what I was doing, because suddenly, everyone and their freaking mothers was an expert on child rearing. The neighbor who dropped by with an aluminum tray of overcooked lasagna had all the answers regarding sleep scheduling and took two full hours to explain them to me. The one with the chicken pot pie informed me that pacifiers had permanently botched her now teenage daughter's teeth. Baked ziti with a side of meatballs explained to me that the less I bathed my baby, the more beautiful her skin would be. My mother-in-law claimed that she knew the best way to soothe a crying infant. Cousins and aunts and uncles and mere acquaintances piped in with their experiences and knowledge concerning spitting up, burping, bathing, and umbilical cords. Even the UPS guy volunteered his views on circumcision. (For the record, he was vehemently opposed. I didn't ask him to elaborate.)

One thing that I decided, on my own and through no consensus from the peanut gallery, was that I would breast-feed my child. Not only was it best for the baby, but also it would help me take the baby weight off, and I needed all the help I could get in that department. Plus, practically speaking, formula was expensive—why spend thirty bucks on a jar of something my body could make on its own? For me, it was a no-brainer. I knew nothing else, but I was *definitely* going to breast-feed. My distant cousin would be *so* pleased.

Unfortunately, it wasn't that easy. In retrospect, it *did* seem a little suspicious that I was able to wear the same exact bras all through my pregnancy. Every single part of me grew right down to my feet, but my boobs remained the same dismal cup size. This is bullshit, I remember thinking: the one part of pregnancy that was worth getting excited about, and I got completely gypped. At least when my milk came in, I'd have real cleavage for the first time in my life. I'd wear low-cut tops and get out of speeding tickets and trouble of all kinds. The prospect got me through the misery of pregnancy. It was also never gonna happen.

Minutes after birth, Lily latched on like a champ—she was a natural; I was told by the experienced nurses that we'd have no feeding issues at all. But no matter how hard she sucked, she couldn't seem to get satiated. They assured me that once we got the positioning down, feeding would be a breeze. So I cradled her in my arms and nursed her. I cross-cradled her. I nursed her sitting up and I nursed her lying down. I even nursed her like a football, despite never having actually held a football in my life. Nothing seemed to work and she became one pissed-off little girl.

To test exactly how much milk I was producing, the home lactation consultant set me up with a double pump, Old Bessie style. I sat on my bed, bottle hooked up to each breast, and cried after an hour when I had less than a few drops in each bottle. Clearly, this wasn't working and all the fenugreek in the world wasn't going to make a difference. Feeling like a complete failure, I started her on formula, sobbing the whole time.

It turned out (much to the dismay of my diehard breast-feeding friends) that formula wasn't really evil. Actually, it proved rather miraculous. Once Lily was actually getting nourishment during feeding time, the hysterics (from both of us) subsided. With a full tummy, she became a much more pleasant baby. She began gaining weight, rather than losing it, and the pediatrician gave her a big stamp of approval. It may not have been what I'd planned, but it definitely wasn't the worst thing in the world. And, I tried to convince myself and the people gasping when I pulled out the Similac, it certainly didn't make me a bad mother.

Plus, bottle feeding wasn't *entirely* awful. I *did* get to eat and drink whatever I wanted without worrying about the repercussions on my baby's tummy. And it left Jeff or my mother or my best friend just as capable of feeding Lily as I was, a fact that made me sad as well as a little bit relieved. Best of all, now that I wasn't feeding and pumping 24/7, I could get out of the house. And Mama *really* needed to get out.

That first trip out of the house, I think I wore pajamas. Even if they weren't *actually* pajamas, I'm certain I slept in them the night before (and, perhaps, the night before that as well). Motherhood gave me the excuse not to give a shit about how I looked, and I took full advantage of that fact. I assumed the public would forgive my confusion over how to use an ATM machine or properly park my car in between two white lines. I *was* a new mother; I had the best excuse out there.

First-time mothers are the easiest people in the world to identify. I never noticed this fact before I was a mother, but after experiencing what they're going through, I find that the breed is just impossible to ignore. And it seems like they're everywhere. Try it: The next time you are at the grocery store or a coffee shop or the bank, take a good look around—I *know* you can spot her. The first-time mother will be in a complete daze, totally oblivious to the spit-up adorning her left shoulder and the stench of exhaustion emanating from her hair. She will have circles under her eyes and be swaying back and forth, even if there is no baby in her arms at the time, soothing herself just as much as her absent infant. She will be drained, mentally and physically, and could cry on command, if you asked her to.

New mothers with older children as well aren't nearly as easy to spot. They aren't as overwhelmed and exhausted as they were the first time around and they aren't stressing over sleep patterns and exactly how much milk their babies are consuming. They have gained the knowledge that only experienced mothers have: the knowledge to *appreciate* their newborns, before they aren't newborns anymore.

But, even more than the ability to relish those fleeting moments, they've gained the wisdom that as trying and monotonous as the constant feeding and burping and changing may be, it's nothing compared to what's coming in the not-so-distant future. It's the dirty little secret of new motherhood that nobody tells you: Newborns are a breeze. Just wait until you have a three-year-old and you'll kill for those early days.

Unless, of course, you have a truly colicky baby. In that case, best of luck. You're pretty much screwed.

Chapter 5

PAYING FOR THE NINE-MONTH BINGE

Mommy Confessions

• Last week, my hairdresser asked how far along I was. I'm not pregnant, but I pretended to be four months. I can never go back there now.

• How did I let myself get to 210 pounds? Oh, yeah. Pregnancy cravings. Eighty pounds of them.

• I'm still trying to lose the baby weight from my twins. They're juniors in high school.

• I'm praying that my son will come out weighing ten pounds . . . I know it will be hell to deliver, but every extra pound is one more I don't have to work to lose.

• I told my husband that we were on a sex hiatus until I lost the baby weight. That was two years ago.

• I miss my pre-kids stomach so much it hurts.

• I miss the crazy concoctions of food I created when I was pregnant: tuna and roast beef sub with onions, jalapeños, chipotle sauce, vinegar, and carrots was my favorite. Subway thought I was out of my mind.

• I'm seriously debating adopting just so I don't gain all that weight.

• Just tried on my prepregnancy jeans four weeks after having my baby. I was sure they'd just be tight, but OMG, I can't even pull them up past my knees. SHIT.

• I don't know why women complain about the baby weight as much as they do. For the first time in my life, I have boobs! And I love every inch of them.

• I am eight months pregnant, but was overweight to start. My husband just called me morbidly obese and I want to crawl under a rock and die . . . if only I could find one big enough.

• Contrary to popular belief among my family, I don't have postpartum depression. I'm just upset about being so freaking fat.

• I'm wearing maternity jeans but I haven't been pregnant in six years.

Despite all the things I loathed about pregnancy, there was one thing about it that I savored. One thing that made all of the misery and swelling and aches and pains worthwhile. One thing that could, perhaps, convince me to suffer through the whole thing all over again for a fourth and final time (well, one thing *other* than the resulting baby, of course). I'm talking about the food. The glorious, glorious food.

Eating all day long was the only thing that quelled my nausea and it just felt so damn good. Pregnancy marked the first time in my life when I wasn't consciously sucking in my gut and it was absolutely liberating. Now, I know, I know it's not medically *necessary* to eat for two, since the baby is the size of a sea monkey for the first trimester, but I did anyway. Actually, I ate for five. I easily could have fed a small village with what I consumed during my pregnancy. Probably for an entire year.

I can't say that I had any particular cravings, because I simply craved *everything*. Bacon and eggs and tuna fish sandwiches topped with potato chips and pizza with extra cheese and meatball subs and chocolate milk shakes. And that was just for breakfast. I visited the food court at the mall and ate my way around the world in a day. The next day, I did it all over again. Personally, I think the whole craving thing is a crock, anyway. I think women always crave particular foods, knocked up or not, and pregnancy just gives us the excuse to indulge rather than deny ourselves. *Finally.* Admittedly, it's not the healthiest way of getting through nine months, but for me, it was the silver lining to an otherwise miserable experience. The Hershey's Kiss–filled silver lining.

With all the vomiting I did, you'd think that I would have gained a modest twenty pounds or so, right? I mean, I was basically an unintentional bulimic. Unfortunately, that was not the case and I gained a whopping sixty-five pounds. Once, while I was shopping for baby clothes around my seventh month, the Korean woman at the dry cleaner fought with me over my due date. "No way you have two more months," she informed me, waving her pointy finger in my face. "You ready to pop now!" A salesperson at a clothing store actually had the audacity to ask me whether I was carrying an elephant. (I wasn't entirely sure I wasn't.)

When Lily was born, I naively packed my semiskinny jeans for the return from the hospital, thinking that once the baby was out, my stomach would shrink right back up. Between the seven-plus pounds she weighed and all of the shit that poured out of me, surely I'd lose at least thirty pounds, right? The other thirty-five would melt off quickly and I'd be back to my prebaby self in no time. Ha.

Sadly, baby weight is just like any other weight, and it's a bitch to lose.

I've seen countless celebrities boasting about how once they delivered the baby, their weight simply melted off like butter. Their bellies are flat again and their thighs, tight and cottage cheese free. The only remnants of a baby are the porn-star boobs pouring out of their red-carpet dresses. Worst of all, they claim that they're so busy running around that they just forget to eat and poof! Baby weight gone and they've never looked better.

Bullshit.

First of all, there is no running around after a newborn. Maybe you'll dash over to them if you hear a loud thud, but certainly not often enough to break a sweat. No matter how large your house, I highly doubt that normal life with a newborn constitutes an aerobic workout. Even in Hollywood.

And how does one forget how to eat? Like, ever? The only time I ever came remotely close to not eating three square meals plus snacks daily was when I was working in an office for ten hours a day, in a cubicle all alone. But babies eat regularly. Toddlers are constantly asking for snacks and meals and treats. Never mind that their plates constantly need to be "cleaned." As a mother you are *surrounded* by food—how on earth is it forgettable?! Unfortunately, losing weight is the simple math of taking in fewer calories than you burn. So, either you're munching on baby carrots all day, working out constantly, or you've become a milk machine and simply aren't eating. Period.

Unless you are that freak of nature whose weight just evaporates, at some point after giving birth, you will catch a glimpse of yourself and barely recognize the reflection. I remember staring in the mirror for almost an hour, feeling a mix of repulsion, fascination, and awe. And then I took a look at the side view and bawled. My stomach was understandable—it had housed a baby, after all, of course it would look like a half-deflated tire. But my ass? There was no excuse for that.

Getting serious after that nine-month-long binge was tragic. I was grumpy and short-tempered and in a constant bitter mood. Mostly, I just missed the seven-hundred-calorie breakfast sandwich I'd become so accustomed to. I'm pretty sure the Corner Bakery missed me, too. But I slaved away at the gym and pretended garbanzo beans and roasted cauliflower were delicious, and I eventually wore those skinny jeans again.

Until the following spring, when I craved that bacon-and-egg sandwich on a fresh croissant. I practically cried tears of joy while eating it and suddenly realized I was at a crossroads. Practically speaking, now was as good a time as any to start trying for another baby, and I was *really* hungry. Plus, my college roommate was getting married that fall and it was either continue starving to fit into the tight dress alongside her miniature high school friends, or be the one waddling down the aisle in a specially altered bridesmaid dress. As I licked grease off of my fingers, the decision was made. Two weeks later I was pregnant and the local pizza shop was once again on my phone's speed dial.

Even though I knew from past experience just how hard that weight eventually would be to take off, I ate my way through nine delicious months all over again. Sixty-five pounds, right on the button. I can't say I have any regrets, though. My Ben was worth every last calorie, just like his brother was less than two years later.

Even if I'm still carrying those croissants around on my ass.

Chapter 6

THE NAME GAME

Mommy Confessions

• I had no idea when I was dreaming up all of my cute baby names growing up that someday I would marry a man who would shoot them all down.

• I wouldn't date a man because his name was Norman. I've often wondered whether he was the perfect man for me and got away for that ridiculous reason.

• I changed my daughter's name at the last minute and totally regret it.

• I refuse to allow my son to be a "junior" in this family . . . the last thing we need is to have a miniature version of his father running around.

• My husband is determined to name our baby girl after his mother. Her name was Ruth. Shoot me now.

• I named my son after a boy I had a crush on in high school . . . my husband has no idea he has a namesake.

• People who choose a baby name but keep it secret from friends and family until the baby is born are just annoying. News flash, Walter Cronkite . . . none of us give a shit.

• My best friend named her son Frederick. I fear he's going to grow up to be just as nerdy as she is . . . but hopefully equally as sweet.

• I let my husband name my daughter and I spend every day regretting that decision. Able Luna. What the hell kind of name is that?

• I secretly love it when people name their children ridiculous names. It gives me something to laugh at.

• I'm dying to tell my sister that the name she picked out is UGLY.

• I want to have another baby just so I can use the girl name I've loved since I was seven.

• Naming a child is way too stressful . . . I'm tempted to have an online vote and be done with it already.

• My best friend just named her son Storm. Is that even a name?

• If I meet one more parent who named their child something that 90 percent of the country can't pronounce, I just might punch them in the face. What happened to Sarah and Jane?

When you are one half of a couple for any decent amount of time, the inevitable questions commence. The distant relatives you run into at reunions, the old English teacher you see at the grocery store, your sorority sisters—they all want to know one single thing: when are you two tying the knot? It's none of their business and it doesn't impact them in the least, but they just *have* to know. And then, once you *are* married, the question moves on to procreating. Have you thought about it? How many children do you want? You never know how long it will take, you know, so you really ought to get started. Go . . . *now!* Quite an aphrodisiac, those conversations.

And then you get pregnant. Congratulations! You waffle about exactly how and when to share the exciting news with friends, family, and strangers alike. Matching T-shirts? Holiday newsletter? Pregnancy test Halloween costumes? An actual bun in the oven? Whatever the announcement, *finally,* the peanut gallery will be satisfied. You can just sit back and bake that baby of yours and they'll shut the hell up. Thank goodness. Except they'll inevitably have one burning question they're just dying to know: what are you naming the baby?

Before I had children, I always found it annoying when people would mysteriously answer that question with "We know the baby's name, but we're not sharing. You'll have to wait." It seemed like such a pompous attitude—the grown-up version of singing "nah-nah-nah-nah-nah-nah." You know the answer to what you are being asked but are refusing to share? When would that *not* be considered rude?

But then I got pregnant and *totally* understood. Once you are with child, unsolicited baby-name feedback can surface a hidden rage deep inside of you. When pregnancy hormones abound, hearing a mere stranger tell you that your baby name is a poor choice serves as a completely valid reason to lose it on them. Cross your fingers for a female judge, because only she would appreciate that this is clearly justifiable homicide. Please, people: if you ask what parents-to-be plan on naming their child, be prepared to respond with "Wonderful choice!" no matter how awful the name. Or be prepared to be butchered. Really, you asked for it.

The day I found out I was having a girl, I made the most important purchase of my entire pregnancy: *The Baby Name Bible*. Aside from a few particular pages in Judy Blume's *Forever* the summer of my eighth-grade year, *The Baby Name Bible* saw more action than any other piece of literature in my entire life, probably more than all the others combined. Jeff and I took it out on dinner dates and thumbed through it while watching TV. I took it to work to devour over my lunch break and it accompanied us on vacations, weekends away, and trips to the bathroom. Countless hours were spent studying it and obsessing over it.

Like most females I know, years and years before I was ready to start a family, I'd picked out the names I would give my future children. Of course, I was young and naive and thought that all that went into a baby name was my own personal taste. Silly me. Once the time actually came, there was so much more that played a role in the decision: the Jewish tradition of naming after a deceased family member, the way names sounded with my married last name, what initials the names formed, what relatives had chosen . . . never mind Jeff's opinion (not that his mattered all *that* much).

For me, a girl's name needed to be beautiful, but not common. Unique and original, but not unheard of. We highlighted the names that we liked in the *Bible* and they were endless. Juliet, Ella, Isla, Mia, Amelia—feminine names were just so . . . *feminine* and we agreed on so many. We could easily name triplets! Octuplets, even. Narrowing them down was agonizing, but once we saw the name Lily, our decision was made. It went perfectly with the middle name we had chosen to honor my grandmother and it was sweet, pretty, and timeless. Unless she grew up to be some sort of butch motorcycle racer, it was highly unlikely that she'd resent us for the choice. What could you hate about Lily? When she was born, the name seemed perfectly fitting and there wasn't a moment of regret. It was the way a baby naming was meant to be.

The experience of naming the boys was an entirely different one. I read *The Baby Name Bible* constantly but found a problem (albeit maybe not the most rational problem) with each and every name in the book. One afternoon, seven months pregnant, I cried to a neighbor about the lack of unflawed boys' names. We're never going to settle on one, I moaned. "How about Benjamin?" she suggested. Benjamin. It wasn't an *awful* name, I thought. The initials didn't combine to create anything laughable or offensive and there were a couple of decent nicknames to choose from. It was totally respectable and classic and I couldn't find a single thing wrong with it. So, two months later, Benjamin it was. A *fine* name.

Everything was peachy until he started preschool a few years later. My heart fell to the floor the first day of class when I skimmed the student list. There, along with my Ben, was not one, not two, but three other children by the same name in his class alone. So much for originality. From that day forward, my boy became Ben S. and I became just another mother who chose the twenty-fifth-most common name for my son. Dammit.

I had learned my lesson. Whatever I did, for my next child I was staying away from the top twenty-five list, which, to my horror, now included my daughter's name. We'd picked out a handful of names for Evan before he was born: Julian, Nathaniel, Caleb, Adrian. But when he was born, he just didn't look like any of those names. I threw the *Bible* at Jeff. "Start looking," I barked, and he obliged.

"Jack?"

"No. Remember Jack and Jill? Are we a freaking nursery rhyme?"

"William?"

"Jesus, Jeff. Jill and Will? C'mon."

"Zachary? Noah? Aiden?"

"No. No. No."

"How about Evan?" Jeff sighed, exasperated.

"Evan?"

It wasn't *terrible*. I didn't *hate* it.

"All right. Evan. I can live with that. I guess."

And so, Evan it was, and Evan it is.

Lily, Ben, and Evan. I think they are nice, solid names, don't you?

Wait.

Forget I asked.

Chapter 7

THE FUR BABY

Mommy Confessions

• I'm terrified that I won't love the baby I'm carrying as much as my five-year-old.

• My first baby signed at ten months old and made every animal sound I asked for . . . my third just turned two and he can't even say "Mommy" yet.

• I had six kids so they'd all be close and take care of one another. Only two are speaking, one lives abroad, and the others have no contact with us.

• I didn't breast-feed my second baby because I didn't want my toddler goggling my boobs.

• I'm pregnant with my second baby and the last thing I'm worried about is whether or not I'll love him as much as his brother. HOW AM I GOING TO LOSE THIS WEIGHT AGAIN?!

• I used to stress out if my first child fell asleep for the night before eating dinner. I'd wake her up just to eat. With this kid, I barely remember to feed her.

• My middle child gets away with everything just because I always kind of forget about him.

Lily may be our first child, but she can't claim the title of being our first baby. That goes to the one and only Penelope, that puppy we brought home upon returning from our honeymoon.

For the four years before the kids came into our lives, every single thing revolved around Penelope. We cut short vacations to be able to come home early to her and got up at the crack of dawn to take her outside. I spent every lunch hour battling traffic just to get home to walk her, because the thought of her being caged up for eight hours was simply too much for me to bear. Her days started out with an hour-long romp at the dog park and they ended with an hour-long walk along the gorgeous streets of Georgetown. In between was filled with games of catch, treats, and doggie cupcakes. Seriously, if I'm ever reincarnated, I hope to come back as the dog of a childless couple in their twenties. That was the freaking life.

Weeks before I delivered Lily, when my hormones were at an all-time high, I remember spooning Penelope on the floor, taking in the freshly bathed scent of her fur. "You'll always be my baby," I sniffed. "I promise, nothing will ever change that."

That was, perhaps, the biggest lie of my life. Since then, *everything* for Penelope has changed.

Now Penelope is still a very well-loved dog, but the pecking order in the family has altered with every baby that enters the household. Her once soft and shiny fur now boasts an odd scent of popcorn and dirt, and I can't remember the last time I actually brushed her. We now take her on walks out of necessity rather than joy, and she hasn't actually played in years. Her leash is coming apart at the seams, and she's lucky if I remember to fill her bowl without being reminded. If I'm ever reincarnated, the *last* thing I want to come back as is the family dog in a household of three young children.

I recall feeling similarly when I was pregnant with Ben. Despite my immediate feelings of ambivalence toward Lily, I had fallen deeply in love with her and she was the center of my universe. Like any first-time mother, I kept track of each and every one of her milestones, celebrating even the most minor events and agonizing over any slight delays. I frequently called the pediatrician's office just to make sure things were normal, and her baby book was updated weekly. During the day, we played and shopped and took classes and had full-blown photo sessions, the results of which I sent to Jeff at work, daily. She was, like any other only child, spoiled rotten with love and affection.

The last month of my pregnancy with baby number two was spent overcompensating for the fact that Lily's days as she knew them were numbered. I wondered how on earth I would possibly love another child like I loved the one I had. I knew, of course, that I was *capable* of loving another one, but exactly how much? Lily was always going to be more than a thousand days older than her brother—wasn't it, logically speaking, inevitable that I would love her a thousand times more? I simply couldn't grasp that it *wouldn't* work like that.

Upon Ben's birth, I realized that there is no shortage of the love a mother has to offer her children. There is a never-ending supply of love, pride, and affection, and each child will no doubt receive his equal share. Thankfully, it's just the way we are built. There is, however, something that each child *doesn't* get the same amount of, and that is called attention.

Considering I now had two children, it made logical sense that Ben would get half as much attention as Lily. But, of course, as I was learning, motherhood knows no logic. The allocation of attention seemed more like 75 percent for Lily and 25 percent for Ben. But he never seemed to mind. He was happy as could be and totally content to just go along for the ride, another spectator in the Great Lily Show. I didn't worry about his milestones like I did with his sister. I knew he would walk and talk when he was ready, and eventually, I was proven right. Instead of a baby book, I got him a monogrammed box where I tossed every keepsake, vowing someday to do more with them. Being as relaxed as I was, I could really enjoy the early days with him, savoring his tiny little feet and intoxicating new-baby smell. I relished the peaceful moments of his tiny body sleeping contentedly and studied his little toes and skin folds, knowing they'd soon not be so very clean and delicious. I inhaled the smell of his neck and tried to memorize his fingers. I loved every minute I stole from his sister.

When Evan was born, I took a little attention from both Lily *and* Ben, providing him with approximately 10 percent of what his siblings got. He exclusively wore hand-me-downs and his stroller and infant carrier had never really been cleaned up from Ben's use, two years prior. I would have been appalled had someone suggested used equipment for Lily, but this round, far more appalling was the thought of buying new merchandise. He had no baby book and I couldn't tell you what his first foods were or when he took his first steps. With Lily, I didn't leave the house with her for weeks, afraid of the germs and the dirt the general public would share with her. Evan made his debut after a matter of days. I just couldn't wait to get out of the house, and he joined me. Guess what? He lived.

For the first two years of his life, the poor boy never owned a new toy. In fact, for his first birthday, I simply replaced all of the batteries in the toys he'd been playing with his entire life and it was like I had infused the house with magic. The toys actually lit up? And sang? And moved? He was spellbound. It was absolutely pathetic. To this day, he remains the easiest to please of my children, literally jumping for joy over matching pajamas.

There certainly are pros and cons to being the first, the middle, and the last of my children, and their personalities have been shaped, in no small part, by the kind of mother I was to them. Lily gets distraught when her smallest achievements aren't applauded and her creations aren't immediately hung for display, clearly a result of my early enthusiasm and encouragement. Ben tends to roll with the punches, much like he did as an easy-to-please little infant. And Evan is very much a last child, constantly performing and clowning around, desperate to get some attention of his very own. But they're all well loved and well cared for and that's what really matters at the end of the day.

Well, except for Penelope. She *really* does need that bath.

Chapter 8

SUBJECTIVELY REVOLTING

Mommy Confessions

• There was a round, brown pellet on the floor. I assumed it was an oddly shaped chocolate chip, but I sniffed it to be sure. Thank God, because it wasn't chocolate at all.

• I'm going on day three without a shower. Sadly, I'm not even dying to take one.

• One of my kids dropped a lollipop on the floor of the grocery store and began to pitch an unholy fit. Just to shut my child up, I picked up the pop, stuck it in my mouth to suck off all the grocery store floor crud, and gave it back.

• I encourage my kids to bite their nails so I don't need to cut them.

• When my son peed the bed in the middle of the night I was so tired that

I just put newspaper down. He never forgave me for that. Hopefully, when I get old, I'll piss my bed and he'll have to deal with it.

• My pediatrician has told me not to, but I just can't help digging ear wax out of my son's ears. It's addictive.

• I suck on my daughter's pacifier to "clean" it off. Not sure it's getting any cleaner, but it makes me feel better.

• I feed my husband food that's fallen on the floor. I figure it's his fault for telling me not to waste money.

• I lost the nose sucker thing and had to suck a booger out so the kid could breathe. I didn't realize what I had done until I spit the booger out and told my husband. He said, "You're a mom now. That's part of the job."

• I still wipe my eight-year-old's bottom. It's so much better than dealing with the skid marks if he does it himself.

• My daughter threw up in my hair last night. I still haven't washed it out.

• I don't think my five-year-old son has been wiping. Oh well. Saves toilet paper.

• I noticed after the diaper change was over and the wipes weren't in reach that there was a little poop on my hand. I just rubbed it off on my jeans and went on with the day.

No matter how well groomed and well coiffed a woman might be before she has children, she transforms into something entirely different as soon as she becomes a mother. Something resourceful. Something impressive. Something . . . disgusting. Motherhood just has a way of stripping away all the girly glamour we try so hard to exude and reverts us back to how I imagine our cavewoman ancestors lived—mud on the face, raccoons for lunch, urine for hydration.

It's part of what bonds us, I think—the grossness.

Mothers think nothing of using saliva to clean our little ones' faces or openly smelling their bottoms to determine whether they've indeed defecated. If our kids swallow a penny, we will weed through their poop to ensure the coin has actually come out the other end, and we will catch vomit with our bare hands if necessary. We pluck off cradle cap from their tiny heads and find deep satisfaction in extracting a dried booger from their noses. Some moms, me included, find it safer to just bite the fingernails of their newborns rather than use scissors, terrified of accidentally cutting their tiny fingers. It's gross, sure, but we have to do it . . . who the hell else would?

I'm a bit of a contradiction where the nasty stuff is concerned. Despite not thinking twice about wiping a wet nose with my bare hands or being kissed on the mouth by a drooly toddler, I just won't do certain things. Drinking after my children, for instance. If Evan and I were on a desert, alone, and the only thing to quench my thirst for miles was a water bottle of which he'd consumed half, I'd rather die of dehydration than sip from that nasty-ass bottle. The child has given me a new appreciation for the word "backwash." I swear, half of what he's consumed for the day comes back up and floats around in his beverage in the form of tiny white flecks. It's revolting.

I know of many moms who habitually finish the food that their kids leave on their plates. Now, I certainly understand why some moms do the occasional grazing on food left on their kids' plates, but I've seen what my kids do to their dinners, and it's the most unappetizing thing in the world. They lick things and sneeze on things and mush them up and push them around, and I'll be damned if I'm going to be snacking on that shit. Even if I *am* actually hungry.

Another thing I would never dream of eating? My placenta. *Of course,* you're thinking, right? I mean, who in her right mind would dream of eating such nastiness? But people do. It's, like, a thing. Women do everything from encapsulating their placentas into vitamins (I wouldn't do it, but at least it doesn't make me dry heave) to mixing them into smoothies (berry surprise, anyone?) to actually chomping on them raw (OMG, hold me; I may never eat red meat again).

I was disgusted enough when the nurse asked me whether I wanted to take the thing home and bury it, but *eat* it? Raw, even? Apparently, it's supposed to help minimize bleeding and depression, in a holistic, crunchy (and unproven) way. For me, I don't think there are many things more depressing than eating an organ that helped in waste elimination and gas exchange for nine months of my life, even if it did also feed my unborn child. If I had to bleed a little more because my placenta ended up in the biohazard box, so be it. I have no doubt that that's where mine belonged.

And despite my enthusiasm for protecting and preserving our environment, you won't find me washing out my reusable maxi pad or laundering cloth diapers. Is it horrible to admit that I might be willing to shave a few hundred years off of Earth's life just to add a few moments of sanity to mine?

Now excuse me while I go dig out some ear wax from my son's ear.

That's the kind of gross I can handle.

Chapter 9

THERE ARE NO SICK DAYS
IN MOTHERHOOD

Mommy Confessions

• Sometimes, I wish I'd catch the flu just so I could stay in bed all day.

• My husband got a stomach bug and dropped thirteen pounds in a week. All I got was an extra kid to take care of.

• I constantly fake menstrual cramps.

• Last week, my husband was so sick we had to get a sitter at 10:00 p.m. for our sleeping child and go to the ER. We were there for FOUR HOURS. The verdict? A cold. Take some Advil. We spent four hours in the ER for a cold. Jesus.

• I called in sick for work, took the kids to day care, saw an afternoon movie, and got my nails done. Best day EVER.

• My husband moans, loudly and incessantly, when he's sick. I'm not

kidding. "Ehhhhhhhhh . . . mmmmmmmmmmmm . . . uhhhhhhhhhhhhh
. . ." The first time he did it, I thought he was messing around. He wasn't.
It makes me crazy.

• I hate the smell of my kids when they are sick.

• I lock myself in the bathroom and act like I have diarrhea, but really
I am sitting in there reading magazines and playing on my phone. My
husband keeps pestering me to see a gastroenterologist.

• I'm sick and all I want is for my mommy to come and take care of me.
I'm forty-seven.

• I love when my kids are sick and I don't have to feel guilty for letting
them watch constant TV and never leave the couch.

• Motherhood is having your toddler throw up nasty fake-grape-smelling
Pedialyte in your hair, lay her head down on your shoulder, and say, "I
want Daddy."

I often fantasize about going back in time in my shiny silver
DeLorean and passing on some words of wisdom to my pre-
mommy self. Of course, that selfish bitch probably wouldn't
listen to a thing I had to say, since she thought she knew everything, but I'd try nonetheless. I'd tell her to sleep in later on
the weekends, because once she has kids, she'll never sleep well
again. I'd tell her to flaunt those spider vein–free legs, use more
moisturizer, and deep condition more often. I'd tell her to eat
her meals slowly, savoring every bite, because soon food will

be consumed out of necessity rather than pleasure. But most important, I would tell her to run to the nearest public restroom and lick the doorknob, or walk up to a sniffly stranger at the coffee shop and inhale his sneeze, or take public transportation and stand uncomfortably close to coughing passengers. However she possibly could, I would tell her to soak up all the airborne germs she could get her healthy little body on. Get sick, girlfriend, I would say. And then milk it. Because once you become a mom, you'll never be able to get sick again.

Of course, mothers get sick. In fact, we are *constantly* sick. How could we not be? We are surrounded by snotty children who are walking diseases for a good portion of the year. They bring home sicknesses we've never heard of from school and from playdates. Winter months are spent wiping snot-filled noses with our long sleeves, until, eventually, we give up and just wear tank tops. The pediatrician's office becomes our home away from home and the pharmacists know us by name. I don't think I have felt 100 percent healthy since Lily was born. It's always something—either a small case of the sniffles or a pounding headache or a full-blown stomach bug. I can't recall what it felt like to get a good night's sleep, and I've just become accustomed to the dull pain in my shoulders and to operating at less than optimal performance level. Children are just synonymous with sickness.

If life were fair, being sick would be the one time a mother could catch a break, the rare instance when she'd be granted time off from the routine of waking up too early and running around after other people and not having a moment to herself. She'd be able to rest for a change. Sip chicken noodle soup, even if she had to make it herself and take a steamy shower alone. Do the necessary things to get better. But, unfortunately, nothing's fair in parenthood and there are simply no sick days in motherhood. *Ever*.

Fathers are entirely different. When fathers are sick, they have the luxury of once again becoming children, except instead of their *own* mothers caring for them, their lucky wives get assigned to the task. There's a reason why the line "in sickness and in health" sneaks into those wedding vows—I can think of no better reason to leave a man than for the way he copes with sickness. Now, I love my husband. I truly believe we are soul mates, my life wouldn't be complete without him, he is the love of my life and all that crap, but when he's sick? I have visions of stabbing him repeatedly with sharp kitchen utensils and making a run for it with our children.

When Jeff has a cold, it's as if the world is ending. He moans and groans and pouts and whimpers audibly. He asks for drinks and the remote and for head rubs. He sleeps on the couch because the poor baby can barely muster the strength to walk up the stairs. He's pathetic. It's all so over-the-top that it would be amusing if I weren't the one falling victim to his evil ways.

Last year, we were both feeling crummy. We went to get checked out, and I was diagnosed with conjunctivitis, an ear infection, and a sinus infection. Leaving the doctor's office, I couldn't help but feel giddy. I had orders—from a *doctor*—to take it easy and rest up. Visions of *Girls Just Want to Have Fun* and *Dirty Dancing* floated in my head. I'd get to nap on the couch and sip milk shakes and actually be waited on for once. Sure, I felt like crap, but it was worth it. *So* very worth it. I was psyched.

An hour later, Jeff came back from his doctor's office visit with a different diagnosis: pneumonia. He was bedbound with a 104 fever and needed IV fluids. All I could think was that the bastard had one-upped me. There I was with eyes swollen shut, nose totally clogged, and ears so full of fluid that I couldn't hear, and I was stuck coddling *him*! To make matters worse, Lily woke up the next day with a fever. I thought about jumping off the roof but then worried that I would survive, ending up paralyzed and stuck wheeling around the kitchen for the rest of my life, making breakfast, lunch, and dinner.

If keeping kids healthy is a parents' job, having to keep sick kids home from school is the cruelest imaginable punishment for a failed mission. My kids go to school, goddammit, unless they are running a fever, puking their guts out, or bleeding profusely. Of course, I also am a frequent visitor to the nurse's office when my morning judgment on borderline sickness proved to be the wrong one. A couple of years ago, I was called in to pick up a tummy-aching Ben from school. As I embraced my green-faced child, I was wracked with guilt: How could I have taken him into class when he'd complained about not feeling well the hour before? What kind of monster was I, choosing grocery shopping and working at Starbucks over nursing my baby back to health? Payback came in the form of buckets' worth of puke exploding on my chest and seeping through my bra. Chunky, curdled puke. I held his hand and did the walk of shame to the car, stinking up the hallways and vowing to keep him home the next time I was in doubt. Not surprisingly, I awoke the following morning with a stomach bug, along with a house full of three vomiting children.

There's simply no way around it: a sick mother gets zero sympathy, but it's just par for the course, I suppose. And one day, when I am old and weak and gray, my kids will take care of me and this all will have been worth it, right?

Right?

Chapter 10

GRILLED CHEESE, SQUARED

Mommy Confessions

• My kids eat the same thing every single day for lunch. I'm sure their teachers think I'm a terrible mom.

• I eat sweets while hiding in the bathroom so I don't need to share with my children.

• The only thing my kid eats is mac and cheese. I'm not exaggerating.

• When my son refuses to eat something because it looks funny, I want to stab my eye. IT'S FREAKING CORN!

• When I am eating my secret stash of M&M's and my three-year-old asks what I'm eating, I say broccoli.

• You know what's worse than kids who refuse to eat vegetables? A father who sets that example.

- We have breakfast for dinner once a week. Okay, three times a week.

- Ketchup is the closest my kids have gotten to vegetables in months.

- I can't blame my son for wanting to eat only chicken nuggets . . . that's all I want to eat, too.

- I claim to be a "natural parent," but my kids and I eat junk food all the time. This morning we had cookie dough for breakfast.

- I sneak boiled veggies into all of my kids' foods. Their favorite chocolate muffins are made with spinach and sweet potatoes. It makes me insanely happy.

- Biggest pet peeve: when my daughter FINALLY agrees to try a bite, takes a TEENSY lick, then determines it's disgusting.

- I feed my kids healthy, well-balanced meals and I eat a bowl of cereal for dinner every night.

There are two types of mothers in this world: those who make one healthy meal for their entire family to enjoy as a whole, and those who cater to their children's palates, serving a kid-friendly option for their little ones and regular food for the adults. There's no question what the right approach is. Obviously. *I* am the type of mother who cooks one healthy, well-balanced meal of protein, vegetables, and a starch, and my entire family gobbles it all up without complaining.

Snort.

That's the kind of mother I was *supposed* to be, at least. The one I am in some parallel, opposite-day universe where I'm also not caffeine dependent and enjoy push-ups and get in daily showers. In reality, my kids eat a separate dinner consisting of things I *know* they'll eat, rather than things they'll simply complain about. (Oh, and for the record, I haven't done a push-up since high school and am usually unshowered. But you probably guessed that.) Somehow, I have become that short-order cook I always vowed *not* to be. The one who has let her children win.

It wasn't always like this. Back when the kids were younger, they were open to trying new foods and enthusiastic about eating what was put in front of them. Salmon! Spinach! Grapefruit! Quinoa! Brussels sprouts! Up until age two, each of my children had enviable palates and I pitied the mother who made grilled cheese sandwiches for breakfast, lunch, and dinner. And then, it happened, shortly after Lily's second birthday. "Here you go," I said as I presented her with roasted beets and goat cheese, one of our favorites. "Yuck," she pronounced, violently pushing it away. "That's gross now." At first, I thought it a fluke. Perhaps, she just wasn't in the *mood* for New American that day; she was allowed to be fickle now and then. But then she also turned down the roasted vegetable lasagna and sweet potatoes and halibut that followed. "What do you want?" I cried. "What is happening?" Her eyes lit up. "Grilled cheese," she pointedly responded. "*That's* what I want." It seems she'd had it the day before during a play-date and the seal was broken. For the next year, the only food that made her happy consisted of white bread and imitation cheese.

Like clockwork, grilled cheese is what each of my children suddenly wanted from two years old on—it's like they were programmed that way, somehow. Grilled cheese *did* expand to macaroni and cheese, peanut butter and jelly, and french fries. Typical kid fare. Even when I try to climb out of the food rut we're in, it's unsuccessful. "This is gross," they cry over the homemade mac and cheese I spent hours shredding and mixing. "We want the *real* mac and cheese, the one in the blue box!" There's nothing like a preference for Kraft to make you feel like a real nutritional failure.

Another surefire way for me to feel like this is by volunteering in the kids' classrooms at lunchtime. Sure, there are the lunches that will make me feel like I'm in good company—the fellow peanut butter and jellies with crusts still intact and bags of grapes and Goldfish. There are even the kids who bring the same Lunchables every day, making me feel slightly better for actually doing *some* bit of assembly at five o'clock in the morning. But then there are the others. The beautiful color-coordinated Tupperware containers boasting last night's leftovers and a rainbow assortment of fresh fruits and vegetables. The bento boxes filled with exquisite little pieces of art, fashioned out of rice, radishes, and berries. The soups still warm in thermoses and crustless, spa-worthy mini-sandwiches. There are some mouthwatering lunches in that cafeteria, but from what I've seen, they're also most likely swapped for a forbidden bag of Doritos.

I keep telling myself that it can't possibly go on like this forever. Eventually, my children will learn that there really is more to life than orange cheese and bread or noodles. There's a whole world of turkey and stuffing and pad thai and bouillabaisse and bacon and frittatas and fish tacos just waiting for them to discover, and I'm quite sure they'll come around.

Until then, though, I'm going to savor the silver lining: their pickiness means more deliciousness for me. So what's the rush?

Chapter 11

THE "PERFECT" PICTURE

Mommy Confessions

• I am always behind the camera, but never actually in the picture.

• My daughter threw up ALL over Santa's lap. The look on his face makes it my favorite picture ever.

• My twins are three and we've still never had a family picture taken.

• To get my kids all to smile for pictures, I burp on command. Always makes them laugh.

• I'm the worst mom in the world: I refuse to order school pictures. Thirty bucks for a terrible, posed shot? No thank you.

• I secretly submit my BFF's Christmas card to the Awkward Family Moments website. I think it would be hilarious if they someday publish her photo.

- I totally forgot that it was Picture Day at school this year. Yes, that is my child with the uncombed hair and unbrushed teeth.

- My husband has about a thousand more pictures with the kids than I do. At least if we both die, they will remember what he looks like.

- I bribe my kids with chocolate to get them to smile for photos.

- I had to Photoshop a family picture together since nobody was capable of smiling at once.

- I'm thirty pounds overweight and too embarrassed to ever get my picture taken. It makes me sad that my kids will never see their mom with them when they were little.

- I'm pretty sure the "perfect" picture is nothing more than an urban legend.

Before I was a parent, I had a long list of things from my own childhood that I vowed to do differently. I was *never* going to sing at the top of my lungs when *my* kids had friends over the way my mom did. I would let *my* kids dress in the trendy clothes instead of the classics, so they didn't end up looking like they were ripped from the set of *Little House on the Prairie* like I did, and I'd allow *mine* to watch the same TV shows as their peers, unlike my own folks with their silly, rigid rules. And then there was the antiquing. The horrible, dreaded antiquing. Much of my childhood was spent groaning about having to pull over at musty roadside antique stores and watching as my parents rummaged, bargained, and purchased their little treasures. It was *so* [insert eye roll] boring and it was, like, *so* cruel that they subjected my brother and me to it. I vowed never, ever to do such a thing to my own children. And, still not having gotten over the torture myself, I've so far succeeded.

But my biggest parenting vow by far was not to photograph my kids incessantly the way my parents photographed me. Most of my childhood memories contain my father, right up in my face, documenting my every move with his camera. It was annoying and embarrassing and I'd be dammed if I did the same thing to my own kids.

Of course, just like my vow never to allow Nerf guns and character T-shirts under my roof, the picture-taking one never had a chance in hell. I'd venture to say that I'm even worse than my father ever was. Lily's first sentence was an adamant "No cheese!" directed toward me as I tried to get the seventeenth shot of her burping her baby doll. But I got the shot! And it's adorable! It will live forever in the pages of her first photo album! If I'm really lucky, *someday* she might even appreciate it, the way I do the endless early pictures of me. I just can't help myself. With the camera, I'm borderline abusive. It's just in my blood.

Lily's first Halloween, I was so anxious to capture her in the precious little ladybug costume that I simply couldn't wait until she woke up from her nap. I practically ripped her out of bed, shoved her in the costume, and plopped her outside for my photo shoot. My ladybug was *not* amused and scowled through every single picture I eagerly snapped. We ended up putting her to bed early, completely missing out on the neighborhood party and on trick-or-treating, which I'd been so excited for, just because I had to go and break the cardinal rule of never waking a sleeping baby. I wish I could say that I learned my lesson that day, but all I learned is that if I don't get the perfect picture the first time, try again the next day. And the day after that. And, if necessary? The day after that, too. My favorite Halloween pictures that year came six days after the actual holiday, from our fourth photo shoot. I'm not going for perfection; I know that with kids, that's an impossible goal. I just want to document our experience. With smiling faces and beautiful lighting, of course.

It's not fun being this photo obsessed, but what is a proud mommy supposed to do? For previous generations, photos simply got stuck in frames or albums for close friends and family to see once or twice a year. These days, we post them to Facebook and tweet them and e-mail them and, if they're *really* good, arrange them to music and share them on YouTube. They're *everywhere,* and they'll live on forever. The pressure is almost too much to bear.

My photo-taking technique has, um, matured the longer I've been a mother. Instead of simply telling them to "say cheese," like I did with Lily, I've gotten more resourceful. I know what works with my kids, and I'm nothing if not dedicated. "Fart!!" I'll yell at them, trying to elicit a smile. "Poop, burp, tushy face," I continue, as they lighten up and start to laugh. "Diarrheeeeeeeeeaaaaa!" I scream. Finally, they collapse into giggles and I snap away. It might not be the most restrained approach, and it might result in some appalled looks from innocent witnesses, but I get my frame-worthy pictures. *Totally* worth it. And mildly psychotic.

Clearly, the school photographers aren't onto my tactics, because without me there to micromanage, my kids' class pictures are always failures. Evan's from this year is the closest to perfection I have seen yet—his smile is authentic and adorable, his hands folded sweetly on the desk, his shirt clean and hair combed. The problem? The enormous booger hanging out of his nose. How did nobody notice that?! Such a thing would *never* have happened on my watch. Neither would the freshly stained shirts, pathetic grimaces, and half-closed eyes of school pictures past. I buy the pictures out of parenting obligation, but it's never a thirty bucks I'm happy to spend. They just don't share my high standards.

Whatever. I'm willing to look like a fool in order to capture frame-worthy images of the people I love most. And while I'm quite confident that my children will one day vow never to torture their kids the way I have them, I'm also pretty sure they'll break that vow once they have kids of their own.

At least, I hope so. I sure as hell don't want to be the one behind the camera in thirty years. I'm exhausted.

Chapter 12

THE MOMMY CLUB

Mommy Confessions

• I have triplets, so why am I lonely?

• I have absolutely nothing in common with my childless friends anymore. When I see one of them on my caller ID, I cringe because I know I will be made fun of when I try to explain why I can't just drop everything anymore.

• I stopped liking my best friend when I saw what a terrible mother she is. Her child is a monster . . . I never would have predicted kids would kill our friendship.

• If I had to give up my husband or my girlfriends, I'd give up my husband in a heartbeat.

• I avoid my best friend's phone calls because she's incapable of talking for less than an hour at a time and I have no hours to spare.

• I go out with my girlfriends every other Thursday night. I swear, it's the only thing that keeps me sane all week.

• Since I've had my baby, I feel like I've lost most of my "friends." Don't have anything in common with them anymore and have no idea how to start making new ones.

• I like my online friends more than my real-life ones.

• I talk to my mom more often than I talk to anyone else . . . when did she replace my girlfriends and how the hell did that happen?

• My best friend does everything perfectly, but she can't control her children. I'm secretly thrilled about this.

• I stopped speaking to my best friend because she had the life that I wanted. I miss her every day.

• My five-year-old has deeper friendships than I do.

• I wish I could be happy for my best friend's amazing children, happy marriage, and perfect life, but I'm too busy seething with jealousy.

• My husband says I am his best friend . . . I love him, but friendship-wise, he doesn't even make my top-ten list.

• I consider my kids to be my closest friends these days. I'm pathetic.

The moment you've birthed/adopted/fostered/surrogated/whatevered a child, you instantly become a card-carrying member of the biggest club on Earth: the Mommy Club. Congratulations! There is no hazing and no pledging and membership is instantaneous and guaranteed. The Mommy Club is overflowing with mothers of all shapes, sizes, and colors, with only one necessary bond: a child.

Sadly, one cannot be a member of both the Mommy Club and the Non-Mommy Club at once. The new mom, having just made the transition, will inevitably try to simultaneously keep both memberships—attempting to play the role of a carefree and unburdened girl to her childless friends and the loving and doting mom to her new mommy friends. Her childless friends won't buy it, though, hearing the cries from a baby in the background of a phone call or smelling the stench of spit-up, buried underneath her perfume during a night out. The new mother's cover will be blown, and her former membership immediately revoked, along with the ability to pee in peace or actually flip through an entire magazine in a single sitting.

The Non-Mommy Club is objectively a much more fun club to be in, with conversations never once containing the words "diaper blowout" or "questionable rash." Long dinners of seared tuna and sushi are consumed along with bottles of wine and pretty pink martinis. Impromptu slumber parties and all-night gab fests are not uncommon and shopping or mani/pedis over lunch are considered a strenuous activity. It's the kind of club you *want* to be in, rather than the one you *need* to be in.

The New Mommy Club, on the other hand, isn't nearly as fun or easy. Though induction is a given, the club doesn't necessarily guarantee companionship, acceptance, or solidarity. There is no orientation to meet fellow members and no quarterly get-together. Every member has one important thing—perhaps the *most* important thing—in common, but that's where the similarities end. Having been knocked up at the same time isn't enough to sustain a decent relationship, as any lonely new mother will eventually learn.

Once I was booted from the Non-Mommy Club, I set out to meet some people in my new club. It wouldn't be hard, I thought. There were millions of women just dying to talk sleep patterns and solid foods with me, along with Hollywood gossip and the best shades of lip gloss. I thought it would be easy and natural to find those people, but I was sorely mistaken—making friends as an adult is *hard*. The last time I'd really sought out new friends, I was working at a job with other young people looking to forge relationships, too. It was just . . . effortless. As making friends should be. Before that, I made friends in college, surrounded by other eager and enthusiastic students searching to find their people, too. This time, though, was different. The other mothers I met seemed to be content with their relationships and I just didn't see any vacancy signs hanging in their windows.

Entering the Mommy Club felt like what I imagined it would have been like coming into a new high school halfway through sophomore year. Except this time we had real babies to keep alive, not just experimental eggs playing the role of child. There were cliques within cliques and figuring out just where you fit in was mind-numbing. Was I an earthy mom, one who would wear her baby and sing the benefits of cloth diapering? Was I an active mom, who insists on sprinting with her stroller rather than taking leisurely strolls around the mall, or who does reps with full baby bottles as if they were free weights? Was I a hip mom, striving to maintain a sense of trends and coolness? Was I a laid-back mom, just letting kids be kids and enjoying the ride? I was lost in a sea of diaper bags, infant carriers, and stretch marks, having no idea where I belonged.

After a few months of loneliness and boredom, I got more proactive. I schlepped my baby to story time and baby stores and playgrounds where there was a high likelihood of running into members of the Mommy Club. If I saw a mother who looked like someone I could be friends with, I'd try to think of possible ways to start a conversation. "Need a wipe?" "A teething biscuit?" "How about them toddlers?!" It was just like dating, minus the possibility of free dinner and sex. Although, at that point, I probably would have considered swapping teams if it meant having a girl to see a movie with on a random Wednesday night.

Back in the Non-Mommy Club, friendships were completely selfish and my criteria were pretty much limited to whether or not I had fun with the person. If we shared the same sense of humor, the same interests, and the same idea of a good time, that was pretty much enough. With kids in the picture, however, there was so much more to consider. Could we survive a trip to the zoo together? To a water park? To an indoor play zone? Were they responsible enough to keep an eye on my kid at the pool? Trustworthy enough to drive them to a playgroup or to keep their sick kids far from mine? And, lastly, could I tolerate their children? A nearly impossible list of criteria to fill.

But I've found them: my Mommy Club friends. The ones who I cry to and laugh with and who help me survive the sometimes impossible days of motherhood. They are neighbors and parents of classmates and old friends who've had children—and bloggers, connected through the computer rather than everyday lives. They've taken years to find and aren't always the people I would have expected, but they are mine. And, it turns out, they're just as good as those Non-Mommy Club friends. Sometimes better.

Chapter 13

THE BIGGEST BABY
OF ALL

Mommy Confessions

• My husband thinks I need to be more patient with the kids . . . this coming from a man who hasn't spent more than two consecutive hours with them EVER.

• I sometimes crush up Midol and put it in my husband's food—it makes him sooooo much easier to deal with.

• I tell my husband we are out of milk so I can run to the store for ten minutes of quiet time. I don't tell him I drank the last of the milk.

• I'm married, but sometimes I feel like a single parent.

• My husband is taking his paternity leave to help me with the baby. He will be here for FOUR months . . . we're on day four and I am already wishing he was back at work.

• I think I should have more say-so over our kids than my husband. I'm the one who did all the work to bring them into this world while he jerked off into a cup.

• I don't complain that my husband thinks he deserves to sleep in every weekend because he works so hard; instead, I spend those morning hours spending his hard-earned money online.

• Sometimes I let my kids sleep in bed with us so I have an excuse not to have sex with my husband.

• If I'd known the kind of father my husband would be, I never would have married him.

• I picked a fight with my husband last night just so I could storm off and lock myself in my room. If he didn't think I was mad at him, he would just keep coming in there every few seconds, asking me for things.

• Sometimes, I am scared at how smart my son is . . . he is only seven and I really think he may be smarter than my husband.

• My husband manages to "sleep through" our hungry infant every night. Last night I pulled all the covers off of him, threw them on the floor, and slammed the door on my way out. He didn't sleep through that.

Last winter, on the coldest day of the year, I decided to take a rare bath. After I was all dried off, I continued the alone time with a face mask and a quick call to a girlfriend. Jeff was downstairs with the kids, and surely, everyone could survive without me for a little while longer. Besides, didn't I deserve a few more moments to myself? From the bathroom, I could hear one of my children loudly banging around in the family room. My precious baby was obviously getting restless. "I'll be down in a few minutes," I hollered, waiting for the green clay to dry so I could wash it off. "But, I neeeeed you," I heard from below. "*Pleeeease* come downstairs!" I ignored the wails as the huffing and puffing intensified. When I finally descended after a whopping fifteen minutes of alone time, I found my baby sulking on the couch. "What were you *doing* for so long?" he wanted to know. "I was so lonely." And there he was—the biggest baby of all. My husband.

I looked around for someone to roll my eyes at, but everyone else in the house was happily occupying themselves by playing alone, independently coloring, or reading. So I looked at the dog. "Seriously?" I asked her. "*This* is what I'm married to?" She sighed and put her head down, obviously in agreement. I was just glad to have a witness.

Jeff's transition from husband to child began immediately after Lily was born. It started subtly—a hint of an outturned lower lip when I'd accidentally fall asleep rocking the baby to sleep, when he and I would normally be together. A pouty face when I suggested that I spend a weekend out of town. And from there it grew, from merely a discreet facial expression into a full-blown personality trait. "You don't pay enough attention to me" and "I think you love the baby more than me" escaped his lips on more than one occasion. The metamorphosis was undeniable. Before my very eyes, I watched as the love of my life had transformed into the last thing on earth I needed: another child.

Unfortunately, unlike the others, this child doesn't seem to grow up. My kids are getting to the age when they don't want public affection anymore; I need to sneak in quick cuddles and hugs when no one else is looking. Usually, they just want an air kiss or a wave hello. Jeff, on the other hand, needs to be touched *constantly*. "Can you rub my temples?" he'll ask, giving me no choice as he inserts his head in my lap. He'll sit thisclose to me, reading over my shoulder as I type and taking up my precious breathing space. Sometimes, I find myself hiding out in the bathroom to get some distance, not from the kids but from him. If he could be carried around in a BabyBjörn all day, he would.

Remember the loss of sleep that's synonymous with having a newborn? Well, I'm still experiencing it, years after the bottles and crib have long been retired. It's not feverish children, middle-of-the-night pleas for milk, or help recovering from a bad dream that's keeping me awake at night. No, it's far, far worse. Jeff's snoring has become such a problem that I am shocked that I don't receive calls from the neighbors at three in the morning, threatening to call the authorities if the noise doesn't immediately cease. It sounds like what I imagine a dying elephant to sound like, if there were a microphone placed in the elephant's mouth. I can hear it when I retreat to the family room couch, an entire floor and three rooms away. People at school drop-off assume that I look like death all the time because the kids are keeping me up at night, and they're right. Sort of.

Then there is his inability to do anything for himself. Make a tuna fish sandwich? But where do we keep the mayo? he'll ask. And the bowls? And the cans of tuna? Put away leftovers that he snacks on until bedtime? Apparently, E. coli is not a concern for him, as food sits out until I notice it and put it away, hours later. Pay a bill? Not unless I were dead. It amazes me that my five-year-old can set up the DVR and get past parental controls, but Jeff can barely change the television station without my help.

The one time I actually did sneak off for a weekend away, I came home to a new member of the family: a puppy. Yes, my husband is actually the man who bought a dog when his wife was out of town. "It's for the kids," he defended himself. "They just fell in love." Of *course* they fell in love, when he drove them three hours to the breeder filled with adorable eight-week-old dogs and told them they could pick one out. Guess who ended up having to walk the dog and feed the dog and bathe the dog and take the dog to the vet? I did, that's who. Of course.

The dog lasted a mere few weeks before I'd had enough. After much debate, we gave him to close friends who were overjoyed to take an undeniably precious puppy. The children tearfully said good-bye, and I promised that when they grew up a little bit and proved how responsible they could be, we would revisit getting another puppy for them. And I'll keep that promise.

Fortunately, knowing my husband-child, that day might never come.

Chapter 14

I LIKE YOU
BEST . . . TODAY

Mommy Confessions

• I have five kids, but one of them is definitely my favorite. I can't help it.

• I cried when I found out I was having a third girl. I just always saw myself with a boy and now I'll never have one.

• I love all of my kids, but my baby boy has a special way of wrapping me around his finger.

• I am terrified that there is no way I will love my unborn son as much as I love my daughter. I just don't think it's humanly possible.

• Sometimes I wonder whether my kids can tell I like my oldest daughter best. She's the only one in the family who likes my cooking.

• After the kids are sent to bed I let my middle daughter get back up to watch cartoons with me. She's the only one whose company I can deal with at night.

• Sometimes I simply can't stand my son . . . he reminds me so much of my ex I could cry.

• If my son wants me to like him as much as I like his sister, then he needs to get a whole lot cuter.

• I know it is politically incorrect for a mother to admit that she has a favorite, but I do. I can't help it. It makes me feel like the worst mother on earth.

• When my daughters ask, "Which one of us do you love more?" I tell them that I love them exactly the same, but it's a lie. I really do love one more than the other.

• My daughter is a complete bitch to me. And she wonders why I favor her brother. Wake up, darling!

• I cried at the ultrasound. Not just teared up, but full-out sobbed. I want a girl so bad I can taste it.

• It kills me that my daughter is a daddy's girl. I'm dying for a son just so someone wants me more for once.

• I have a favorite child and I am hardest on him because I feel so guilty about it.

• I love my kids to death. Is it wrong that I don't like them most of the time?

• There is no favoritism in this family . . . Today, I can't stand all of my kids equally.

I have a favorite child. There, I said it.

There is one child of mine who I want to spend more time with than the others. One child whose voice is more melodic than the rest and whose touch is somehow softer. One child who isn't grating on my nerves or instigating sibling fights or tracking in mud over my newly cleaned entryway carpet. One with whom I just seem to be simpatico. Simply put, one I just like more than the other two.

For now.

See, this favorite child of mine changes by the day. No, by the minute, actually. Who is this favorite child of mine? It's the particular one who is pissing me off *least* at any given moment in time. They have all had their fair share of being the favorite and they have all inspired the "Oh my God, did I really give birth to you" moments as well. It's one of the best things about having more than one child: there's always another one to go to when one of the others is driving you up a fucking wall.

I never wanted boys. For some reason, I saw myself as a mother only of little creatures dressed in cute little pink bloomers and polka-dot ruffled bathing suits. I think I've just never particularly *understood* boys, so the notion of raising them seemed foreign and daunting. When I found out at twenty weeks that Ben was a boy, I cried. There, in the office with the ultrasound tech who'd just pronounced that our baby had one beating heart and ten fingers and toes, I burst into tears. Not water-gently-welling-in-my-eyes tears, but ugly tears. Borderline hysterics, like there was something wrong with my child. It was my gut instinct and not one I'm proud of. It was also a surefire way to feel like the ultimate mother failure before my child was even born. The thought of having a boy just terrified me, and I wasn't sure I could possibly love him as much as I loved my Lily.

But something amazing happened when Ben arrived; I fell in love with him at first sight. Unlike the feelings of confusion and fear I experienced with Lily, I had that instant rush of love for my newborn child. Just like in the movies.

Not only did I love him, but I actually *liked* him, too. Lily was the light of my life and I had adored having her to myself for the last two years, but OMG, suddenly she had become a tad annoying. Maybe it was the new baby, maybe it was our recent move, or maybe it was just part of being two years old, but girlfriend *knew* how to assert her independence. The tantrums had started and the drama level at our house was climbing into uncharted territory. My new baby, on the other hand, was happy to just be along for the ride. He ate well and slept well and always had a serene smile on his face. He was a *pleasure*. Who could blame me for falling asleep while rocking him once in a while just so I didn't need to put Lily to bed?

When Evan was born, I had a similar experience, except there were *two* other kids at home. Two kids who had their ups and downs and were developing into real people with real opinions. Otherwise known as pains in the ass. In contrast, Evan was just so . . . peaceful. That's the thing about babies that you appreciate more every time. They may cry and fuss, but they also shut up relatively easily. He quickly became my favorite, especially when the other two were bickering over which cartoon to watch or just how many more chips one had than the other. I inhaled his new-baby smell and retreated to the couch to cuddle him, trying to block out the hysterics in the next room.

These days, there is no consistently easy child. Lily, my lovely and beautiful firstborn, is most definitely the girl I always wanted. She loves her Barbie dolls and playing with my makeup and trotting around in my high heels. We love getting our nails painted together and she's already far surpassed my hair-braiding abilities. It's so much fun watching her play with the same things I played with at her age and relating to her so closely. She's so incredibly sweet and nurturing and, really, the experience is even *better* than I thought it would be. She makes me proud every day. She's my *favorite*.

Unfortunately, there is another girl inhabiting my daughter's body who is far less enjoyable. She's volatile and bratty and, sometimes, I wonder if she has a screw (or fifty) loose. This child likes to yell at the top of her lungs and slam doors with such force that the whole house shakes. She pinches her brothers when nobody is looking and rolls her eyes so harshly that I sincerely worry that they will actually get stuck in the back of her head. She's argumentative and antagonistic and just plain nasty. I'm *really* not fond of *that* girl.

So, it's on to my Ben. My Ben, who already is one step ahead of the rest simply by virtue of resembling me the most. Ben, whose smile lights up his entire face and who can't resist stomping in every puddle he sees. Ben, whose laugh is just contagious and who's always good-natured. He's kind and generous and just an all-around great kid. He's my *favorite*.

But then he whines. Ben's whine has to be the most irritating noise on the planet. His whine could be used as a torture method to drag out top secret information from the most threatening of men. It's constant and shrill and, really, just can't be properly conveyed on paper. You have to hear it to believe it, which for your sake I hope is never the case. When he's in the middle of going on and on about dinner being yucky or a museum being boring or a walk being too long, I often want to shoot myself. At those times, he's most definitely not my favorite.

And then there's my baby. I'm pretty sure Evan will still be my baby when he's forty. Or thirty-five, at least. He tells me he loves me a hundred times a day and melts me every single time. He sings along to every song he knows in the cutest, deepest little-boy voice ever. The things that come out of his mouth completely crack me up and he is so delicious that I could eat him up. Though I resented every minute of my pregnancy with him, I couldn't possibly love him more. Our family would be incomplete without his addition. He's my *favorite*.

But lately, he's begun to be a bit of a nightmare. The kid who used to proudly get himself dressed every day now insists that I outfit him from head to toe. The child who would, at one time, happily eat salmon and peas now wants only peanut butter and jelly sandwiches for every single meal. His newly begun tantrums rival any other tantrums I've ever seen before and he's a walking incubus, ensuring that our winters are spent running back and forth from the ER to the pharmacy and back home again. When he's thrashing around on the floor over not being allowed a third breakfast bar in an hour, I crave a more reasonable child. A more mature child. A child whom I can reason with and converse with like a sane human being.

So, I find Lily. And she's my favorite again. For a bit.

It's the cycle of multichildren motherhood and I really don't feel guilty about preferring one to another in the least. I love them all and they're each the golden child at *one* time or another, so it all evens out. Besides, who *wouldn't* prefer a child who is behaving like himself rather than acting like a raging lunatic? It's only natural.

Plus, it makes it easier for me to understand when they pronounce Daddy their favorite parent and tell me that I'm the worst mother in the world. Deep down, I know that *I'm* their favorite.

Just like they all are mine.

Chapter 15

I HATE OTHER PEOPLE'S KIDS (NOT YOURS, OF COURSE)

Mommy Confessions

• I make faces at other people's misbehaving children in the grocery store when their parents aren't looking.

• My best friend's kids have ruined our friendship. I just can't bring myself to be around them.

• My nightmare job would be a preschool teacher. I'd rather collect garbage or clean toilets than be around a bunch of two-year-olds all day.

• I always thought I wanted to be the house where all of my kids' friends convene. Now I am that house and it's totally overrated.

• Why are other people's kids so much more annoying than my own?

• I don't like some of my nieces and nephews and I seriously can't stand having them at my house.

• I "accidentally" tripped a child on the playground yesterday.

• When my kid talks in baby talk, I think it's adorable. When other kids do, I just want them to speak proper English!

• When I read with kids at school and I see disgusting fingernails that need to be clipped with dirt under them, I want to vomit.

• Playdates are just another word for babysitting. Hated it then, hate it now.

• I wish I could handpick my children's friends. Their taste in people is highly questionable.

• I blatantly favor certain children when I volunteer and it's all based on whose parents I can't stand the most.

• My daughter gets picked on at recess . . . deep down I just wish she would teach her bully a lesson by punching her square in the face.

• I don't want to vote for your kids in the "cutest kid" contest on Facebook because, honestly, your kids are not that cute.

• I hate my friend's sticky-fingered minions . . . damn little carpet trolls. I also hate the fact that she thinks it is okay to let them run rampant in my home, which is NOT snot-tot-proof.

• I'm sick to death of feeding faces that don't belong to my children.

• I keep trying to sabotage my daughter's friendships. I know who's better for her than she does.

• I think other people's babies look like aliens. Mine, of course, were the most gorgeous creatures on earth.

I don't like kids.

There, I said it. I'm a mother of three children and mine are the only grubby little snots on the planet whom I can remotely tolerate. Sometimes, I can't even tolerate them. But I digress.

I *want* to like other children. I *want* to kneel down on the ground and ask them questions, the response to which I really care about. I *want* to enjoy having a house full of kids not belonging to me and not glance at my watch every five minutes during playdates. I *want* to, but I just don't. I just can't.

As a teen, I babysat here and there, but I was hardly worth the five bucks an hour they paid me. Sure, I was responsible enough, but I never went above and beyond. I was far more interested in what was on TV once the kids passed out than participating in tea parties or getting them to eat their broccoli and carrots. Babysitting was simply a way to make some extra money, nothing more. The kids may have been cute, but I didn't really feel connected to them the way other people seemed to. They were impossible to understand, they smelled funny, and they were demanding. I did the job I was paid to do, but that was it. It simply wasn't my thing: There were kid people and non-kid people. I was the latter.

I always assumed that something would click inside of me once

I had offspring of my very own. Mothers always seem to have that earth mother–y something or other that allows them to lovingly kiss mystery cuts and scrapes or change poopy diapers belonging to children who share none of their DNA—without dry heaving. It's pretty universal, it seems: Once a child travels through the birth canal or adoption papers are passed, women suddenly become maternal. Like magic. That's the way it works, right?

Well, not for me.

I remember venturing out to the pediatrician's office for that first well-check with each of my new children. There, in droves, were my worst nightmares come to life. I instantly understood what all this "stranger danger" talk was about—these strangers were completely hazardous! Suddenly, instead of being simple annoyances that interrupted my quiet lunch or came to my door selling unwanted cookies, the children were threats, plain and simple. Threats to *my* baby.

The children immediately breathed their foreign breath way too close to my healthy bundle of new joy. I visualized the germs flying over to our infant seat in slow motion, traveling across time and space to where my well baby was innocently sitting, her healthy days now clearly numbered. Did the pediatrician's office really think a single wall was enough to separate the sick kids from the well babies? Had they not heard of airborne diseases? What kind of doctor was this, anyway?

The strange children played with the decade-old waiting room toys and mouthed grungy hardback books and talked gibberish way too loudly. They had dirt under their fingernails and snot dripping down their faces and dried, crusty food circling their mouths. It was like these little scumbags had made it their sole mission in life to sicken my poor child.

But what could I do, build a bubble for my sweet baby? Never venture out into a world filled with creatures whose mission was to destroy her? Live an existence void of stomach bugs, eye infections, and mysterious rashes? *Yes,* that's exactly what I could do! I would build a bubble. A bubble with cozy bedding and sweet-smelling candles and the best pizza delivery. It would be perfect. Did Lily really *need* to interact with other children? Early socializing was *so* overrated—we did have a dog, after all. It'd be like a social survival experiment!

Alas, a bubble we could not live in, especially once I discovered the joys of preschool. I quickly became pregnant with another baby and my need for help with Lily trumped my desire to keep her away from those mutts. The fact that I could ditch my kid for a few hours and shower in peace? *Alone?* Pluck my eyebrows without an audience? I could take a nap and eat lunch while flipping through a magazine, surrounded by nothing but peace and quiet? I was in. And my poor child suffered the injustices of being surrounded for three hours a day by other children.

There was the punk who gave Lily pinkeye the day before her much-awaited first ballet recital. There was the little shit who passed on rotavirus as we prepared for a move from Washington, DC, to Chattanooga, Tennessee. We proceeded to leave soiled onesies at every rest stop for the ten-hour-long ride. And then there was the "friend" who unloaded the little bugs living in her long, blond hair, resulting in a weeklong effort to rid our heads and house of lice.

Unfortunately, the list doesn't end with an itchy head and explosive diarrhea. Last year, a neighborhood kid who was having dinner at our house proclaimed red sauce to be "gross." "It looks like blood," he whined as all three of my children's eyes widened. The obnoxious observation resulted in my children not eating Italian food for months. Italian food, a staple in our diet and one of the few ways I was able to sneak in things like spinach and cauliflower. I swear, every time I saw the kid walking up and down the block, I wanted to dump a jar of Ragu on his head. I'll show you gross, kid. Open wide.

And then there's the "stuff." The older the kids get, the more stuff they need. And where do they learn about this stuff? The other kids, of course. The other kids are the ones who taught my daughter that princesses were dumb and Hannah Montana was where it's at. She heard about *High School Musical* while she was still content watching *Arthur,* and overnight, the Kidz Bop CDs were declared babyish. Taylor Swift replaced the Broadway classics and hundred-dollar UGG boots topped her must-have list for the first day of school.

See? Other people's kids are just useless, bad influences who play no necessary role in our lives.

My children, on the other hand, are *never* the ones to teach the bad habits or pass on germs or do anything the least bit offensive. They are as perfect as they could possibly be.

Well, close to it.

There *may* have been that one time a few years ago, when Lily learned the phrase "Fuck it!" She picked it up from yours truly as a bowl of freshly made fruit salad shattered on the floor. For a few weeks, it was all that came out of her mouth. Honestly, I don't know why those other parents were so worked up when she started using it at preschool. I can see no better reason for the phrase than a spilled paint tray or flyaway paper. She used it in the *perfect* context and the age of three is as good a time as any to be introduced to the word. It's a great word! Personally, I find it bizarre that the kids had never heard it before. Do they live under rocks? I mean, really.

And then there was that time Evan took off his diaper and ran around a furniture store peeing on the floor as other children gawked and giggled. Surely, they learned nothing from the experience. I can't imagine any of them pulled similar stunts later that afternoon.

My kids *might* have started a trend of mooning one another and it *may* have spread across school, but what's a little good, naked fun? It's cute, right? A classic!

And when Evan passed on the stomach bug, he'd clearly picked it up from somebody else's kid. And really, with all the crap those punks eat, a cleanse may have been just what the doctor ordered. I bet the class came out of the whole experience feeling lighter, refreshed, and having gained great mental clarity!

Or not.

So, maybe my kids aren't that perfect after all. I can *kind of* see how some other parents might find them the slightest bit offensive. They do yell a tad bit too loudly and they really aren't all that great at listening. They have been known to spit on a child or two, and Evan *did* once mistake a child for a sandwich. They *may* have even passed on a bad trait or two. But they're mine. And I believe that they are as close to perfect as three kids can possibly get.

I guess all that really matters is that we love our own children and are able to tolerate the rest, for their sakes.

Knowing deep down that ours are far superior, of course.

Chapter 16

THIS "VACATION" SURE IS
A LOT OF WORK

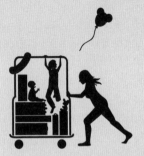

Mommy Confessions

• My middle is two and a half and I'm still not paying for her seat on a plane.

• If I could afford it, I would just pay someone to go on vacation with my kids.

• There are times when driving our car into a tree in order to get my kids to stop arguing in the backseat seems like a good idea.

• I've put potty-trained kids in a Pamper just to avoid the stop and promised candy to them if they agree to actually pee in it.

• Our best friends invited us to their beach house for a week. The idea of being around their kids 24/7 is actually worse than being home alone with mine.

• Laundry from our vacation has been giving me dirty looks all weekend. I think I will just move it into the garage.

• If Disneyland is the happiest place on earth, why am I dying to go home already?

• I have no interest in taking my kids on vacation with me. They stay home with Grandma while my husband and I finally have alone time. So much more fun.

• I intentionally forget toys on road trips so that my husband will agree to a toy store stop to buy a couple of things to keep them busy for the rest of the ride.

• I stop at McDonald's just to use the toilets and the play gym but then feed the kids Uncrustables I brought from home.

• If my son asks "Are we there yet?" one more time, I swear I'm going to knock him out.

• My best friend chastised me when we bought an SUV with a DVD player. She just took her first trip without one with her family and I sang "I told you so" for the whole week after.

• Just got back from a weeklong vacation away with my family to realize I'm not in a single picture. Was I even freaking there?!

• We can't afford to take the kids on vacation. Okay, so we can afford it, we just don't want to.

• I drug my kids with Benadryl on long flights. It's the only way I'll ever travel with them.

• Dear TSA: I know your limit on liquids is three and a half ounces, but for the love of fucking God, do you really think my kid's four-ounce container of apple juice is really a threat to national security?

There are a million things I wish I'd done before I had children. I wish I'd slept in until noon on the weekends, lazily eating breakfast in bed and relishing the fact that I had nowhere to be all day. I wish I'd taken adult classes that really interested me, not just the ones I had to take in order to graduate years before. I wish I'd seen more midday movies, had more spontaneous sex, and read more books, back when I actually had the spare time to do all of that stuff. And I wish I'd appreciated the little things, like the ability to grocery shop or shower when I felt like it.

But perhaps my biggest wish is that I'd vacationed more. Jetted off to Paris last-minute on a dirt-cheap flight. Hopped into the car with Jeff and driven to some bed-and-breakfast in a little town I'd never heard of. Taken the train to New York City for dinner and a show when no local weekend plans materialized. It was just so easy back then to do that, something that became abundantly clear when it wasn't just the two of us anymore.

Once my children entered the picture, traveling went from being a fun adventure complete with tropical drinks and poolside dining to a more exhausting version of being at home. Sure, vacations still provide a change of scenery, but they also are as physically draining as giving blood, and sometimes just as fun.

Family vacations leave me needing a break *from* my break once I arrive back home. Call it a family trip or family getaway or family bonding time; there is really no such thing as a "family vacation." The last thing I've ever felt while traveling with my family is relaxed or rejuvenated.

Gone are the days of simply throwing a few changes of clothes and makeup into an overnight bag and hitting the road. In fact, I am the *last* person I think about when packing. The kids need clothes for each day and backup clothes for each day and layers so they don't complain about being too hot or too cold and is that all I brought because OMG suddenly they *hate* that shirt and why didn't I know that?

They need their toys and their games and their toothbrushes and their pillows and their books and whatever else they simply can't live without while being away from home. My toothbrush and face wash, however, inevitably remain left on the sink so I can end up using hotel bar soap and the kids' watermelon toothpaste.

Because of the abundance of crap that accompanies my children, I find driving to our vacation destination to be far easier than flying. Sure, I'm stuck in the car with stir-crazy children for hours at a time, but at least in a car, we have the ability to pull over for a rest break or an extra dose of Xanax. The kids watch endless movies on the built-in DVD player and we chuck candy back at them to buy moments of peace. In the car, only Jeff and I are impacted by the "Are we there yet?"s and the "She's repeating me!"s. At least the torture is contained.

When we fly, however, we are exposing countless unsuspecting men and women to the hell known as traveling with my family. If you've ever flown with small kids, you know the look of fear in the eyes of fellow passengers at the airport. "Are they on my plane? Please, God, don't let them be on my plane." You can almost see the little speech bubbles hovering over their heads. It's as if they think that if they don't acknowledge you, you won't share a row with them once aboard.

That's if you ever even get on the plane. First comes TSA security—otherwise known as God's "Fuck you" to mothers. Getting my kids through security is a cruel joke, and if you've ever tried to fold up a stroller at the security checkpoint, you know what it feels like to be THE MOST ANNOYING PERSON IN THE SECURITY LINE EVER. The people huffing and puffing in line behind you act as if you're enjoying yourself.

Actually being on the plane, though, is by far the worst part of traveling. I'm held hostage by my kids in flight, knowing that at any moment they could snap and turn every passenger and flight attendant against me. My kids are hard enough to stomach on the ground, never mind at thirty-five thousand feet in the sky. Drugs, junk food, iPhone—I don't care. I just want them quiet and contained. At least until landing.

Finally, assuming nobody's suitcase is missing or we haven't been detained for unruly behavior, it's on to the actual "vacation." Time for a melody of "I'm bored" and "Why are we here" and "He's touching/pinching/yelling/crowding/repeating me" all to the tune of a few thousand dollars. Sure, there are some wonderful moments thrown in there, too, but I always wonder whether they'd have just as much fun at home.

My choice vacation spot before children was the most relaxing place on earth: the beach. A book, a bottle of suntan lotion, a blanket, and I was set—it was the most low-maintenance way I could possibly spend a day. With kids, though, a day at the beach requires more preparation than the SATs. My beach bag is overflowing with snacks and lunch and drinks and toys and cover-ups and sunscreen and towels and blankets just to ensure an hour or two of fun in the sun. Sadly, our definitions of fun differ greatly. I mean, really, is there anything less worthwhile than digging a freaking hole? Try as they might, they're never *really* going to reach China. What's the point? I don't get it. But at least a hole keeps them occupied, which is far more preferable to when they insist on dragging me into ice-cold water along with them. The water is meant to be enjoyed from afar, kids. Duh. As if the beach itself isn't rough enough, it seems to haunt us for days after. I'm still not quite sure exactly how sand ends up in every last orifice, but my children's ear canals are always well exfoliated after spending a day on the sand.

The good news is that a family vacation always brings me a renewed appreciation for my boring home life. When I walk back into my own house, the previously annoying broken hall light seems almost charming, the still dirty dishes in the sink just seem familiar, and the unmade beds beckon us. Home sweet home; it's where we belong and I'm so glad to be there. Until I unpack all of the dirty laundry and cry for another vacation.

This time, one without the kids.

Chapter 17

FREEDOM OF SPEECH

Mommy Confessions

• My son taught the term "motherfucker" to his whole preschool class. He learned it from hearing me refer to my brother-in-law as such. Whoops.

• My kids know all the words to every Eminem CD.

• I'm a good Christian girl, but I can outcuss the best of 'em.

• I told my daughter to shut up yesterday. I can't believe I did that.

• My eighteen-month-old still can't say "Mommy," but used the word "shit" in perfect context today.

• When my mother-in-law criticized my parenting for the umpteenth time, I lost it and told her to shut the fuck up in front of the entire family. I know I shouldn't have but, damn, it felt good.

• My kid was imitating me today. "Slap my ass," she yelled, and I suddenly realized I didn't imagine the figure in the doorway last night as my husband and I did the deed. OMG.

• I think it's hysterical when my four-year-old swears. I know it's horrible, but I just can't help myself.

• "Dammit" sounds really cute when coming out of my two-year-old's mouth. Don't ask me how I know that, I just do.

• I swear at my kids in German and they have no idea what I'm saying. It's awesome.

• My husband taught my son to say "hot, sexy mama" to every woman he sees. It's mortifying and completely unamusing.

• My kids repeat 95 percent of what I say. Especially the bad stuff.

I swore quite a bit before I had kids. I'm not sure why, exactly, but for as long as I can remember, I've had a great affinity for those nice four-letter words. They're just so expressive and instinctual and, frankly, quite fun to use. I naively thought that when I had kids, my language would somehow clean up, but instead, I found that parenthood gave me much more of a reason to curse. I mean, really, what was I swearing about before, anyway? Traffic? A zit? A broken nail? Spilled milk? Puh-lease.

Once I became a parent, only then did I *really* have something to swear about.

Is there anything more curse-worthy than a peed-on top

bunk on the night of the day you actually washed the sheets? Or a toddler thinking it's fun to pour a full bottle of my expensive Moroccan hair oil down the sink? Or an attack of the black Sharpie marker on our brand-new couch? I think not.

"Oops!" just isn't adequate for a middle-of-the-night step on a tiny Lego left on the bathroom floor. "Cripes!" doesn't roll off the tongue when a child dumps his entire uneaten plate of dinner on the kitchen floor, and "Gosh darn it!" doesn't quite cut it when the weather forecaster calls for a sixth snow day in a row. "Fuck! Goddammit! Shit!"

They're all just so much more fitting. And so much more fun to say.

With children, I also have something to swear *at*. Though I would never dream of cussing my children out audibly to their faces, I find swearing in my head to be a highly effective parenting tool. When Lily is screaming that I ruined her life by taking away the hot-pink hair dye that came with her Moxie doll, which was staining the entire first floor of my house, I *may* just see the words "Shut the fuck up" float over her head in my imaginary commentary of the scene. When Evan is thrashing on the floor because I didn't let him have a third bag of Goldfish before lunch, singing a little ditty in my head that goes "Shut the fuck up, you pain in my ass; shut the fuck up, my dear" somehow makes the moment more bearable. And Ben's incessant whining can be blocked out by my silently asking, "Are you ever going to shut your little fucking mouth, you annoying child?" Logically, I know the answer is "not likely," but just asking in my head always makes me feel better. It also makes me a hell of a lot less likely to lose it on them. I like to think of it as a parental coping mechanism. Truly, it works.

I've heard some parents say some pretty awful things to their kids under the guise of constructive criticism. "Don't you think that shirt makes you look fat?" one parent asked her seven-year-old daughter on the playground. Then there was the time I heard a mother tell her son that he was "just like your father," which wouldn't have been a problem had she not kicked Daddy out of the house one month earlier. I even once heard a mother refer to her daughter as "not that bright," while the kid played right in front of her. Personally, I find language like that far more harmful than an occasional "fuck" flown around my house. There are simply no circumstances when words like "fat" and "dumb" and "ugly" are acceptable when directed toward a child. A word like "shit," on the other hand, is just another word for poop. Really, what's the emotional harm in that?

So, from my perspective, a swear word here and there is no biggie. They're just words, after all, not like the stinging judgments that these parents' kids will live with forever. I like to think that I'm making my kids immune to four-letter words, or at least creative in their use of adjectives. In a few years, when the rest of the kids are swapping dirty words at the playground, mine will simply scoff. Giggling over the word "shit"? Amateurs, they'll think. What's the big deal?

And I'll be so fucking proud.

Chapter 18

BIRTHDAY WARS

Mommy Confessions

• I throw my kids' parties more for myself than my children. I really don't care much what they actually want.

• I don't even tell my kids they were invited to certain birthday parties because that's how much I hate going.

• People who spend thousands of dollars on pony rides and bounce houses and designer favor bags make me nauseous.

• I regift for all of the school parties. I'm sure I've given a gift to the person who originally gifted my child with it.

• I hate parties where I have to stay with my child. I think that if someone is throwing a party where extra hands are needed, THEY should provide them.

• If I have to go to one more Little Gym party, I may go postal.

• I miss weekends that didn't revolve around parties for little kids I can't stand.

• I never remember to RSVP for birthday parties until the day before. Not sure why it's so hard for me to remember to.

• To the mother who showed up to my son's party without RSVPing AND with a sibling: I wish I had slammed the door in your face. Rude much?

• I think birthdays should be less about celebrating the birth of the child and more about celebrating the fact that we succeeded at keeping them alive for another year.

• I never spend more than five bucks on birthday presents. It's my dirty little secret.

• I decline party invitations for my daughter because we can't afford to buy the presents.

• I hate parties where the whole class is invited. I don't want to spend the money on a gift for a kid my child doesn't even necessarily play with.

• Birthday parties are the bane of my existence.

I am not a competitive mother in the least. I don't give a shit what your kid scored on his latest math test or what belt he's achieved in karate. If you can bake cupcakes from scratch that rival the very best bakeries, more power to you and I'll devour them without obsessing over my own baking failures in the slightest. I'm a Betty Crocker mom and that's fine by me. You have your strengths, I have mine, and I don't see us as rivals. Ever.

Except when it comes to birthday parties. Where my children's birthday parties are concerned, I want to kick your ass. And I want to kick it *hard*.

Now, I fully realize that I am breaking one of my self-imposed rules not to compete. I recognize that I am *completely* over the top where birthday parties are concerned and it's not healthy or admirable in the least. I'm working on it, I swear. In my defense, I'm pretty sure I inherited it from my own parents. See? It's genetic. Not my fault.

Back in the day, my parents were known for throwing me some pretty kick-ass parties. Fortunately for them, my birthday is just days away from the Fourth of July and all of its celebratory goodness. Yup, I grew up thinking that the fireworks and parades and the whole red, white, and blue shebang was just for me. I kind of still do.

As a summer birthday, the options were pretty endless. We had parties on the beach and at playgrounds and on boats. I celebrated them at camp and on summer vacations and in tents. Whatever they were, they always had one thing in common: awesomeness. One of my favorite birthdays was at home in our backyard and included clown entertainment and a special visit from the local ice cream truck. At six years old, having the singing truck pull up and offer us whatever kind—and number—of frozen confections we wanted was pretty much the coolest thing ever.

And then I grew up, and birthdays stopped being all that

magical. Somehow, they became just another day on the calendar, which, before the days of Facebook, went by without all that much recognition. It's a sad, sad day when you realize that not everybody cares about your big day as much as you do. And then you have kids and suddenly you can live vicariously through them and their *big* days. It's like a whole other childhood!

Unfortunately, I didn't have it as easy as my parents and am cursed to have three winter-born children. I consider it my punishment for not practicing thorough birth control. If I had, I would have three little spring bunnies with countless options for their yearly celebrations. Instead, I am now punished for the rest of my birthday party–throwing life.

I'll sum it up for you in three words: winter birthdays suck.

I'm sorry if you *have* a winter birthday. Not for offending you with the last sentence, but because you have suffered such injustice your entire life. It's just not fair. I feel for you. I *know*.

Unfortunately, there are very few options for the poor winter birthday souls. I long for parties at farms and parks and fields. Do those spring, summer, and fall folks have any idea how very lucky they are? Between the cold and the snow and the short, dark days, winter celebrations are relegated to crappy indoor locations. Topping the list are places like Chuck E. Cheese's (God forbid) and the completely unoriginal gym franchises where 90 percent of child birthdays are held. They have inflatable bouncy things and pimply-faced teenage workers and stink of sweaty feet. They are also the easiest and most sensible option in existence. Fail-proof, you might say. But, like all things in life that seem to make the most sense, I resist them with all of my might.

When Ben turned five, he had the audacity to ask for one of "those" parties. Not only did he want an indoor gym party, but he requested an unoriginal superhero theme. Where was the creativity on that one? A trip to Party City and a scan of the credit card was hardly a party I wanted to put my name behind. He even spotted a large Spider-Man sheet cake at Costco and expected me to put in an order for it. *Costco,* for crying out loud! That's what *other* mothers did. Not me. I hand-designed and addressed invitations and painstakingly assembled professional-looking goodie bags. I baked three-layer cakes and added sprinkles one by one for the perfect color balance. The party he wanted was simply too . . . easy. I successfully talked him out of the Bounce Zone party and into a special kind of hell. A hell otherwise known as the Home Party.

When children are babies, the Home Party is a totally acceptable option. The party consists mostly of grown-ups anyway, and it makes the most sense for your sensitive baby. The birthday boy or girl can change clothes as many times as necessary and easily go down for a nap when the time comes. Home is by far the best place for the unfortunate first-birthday screamfest or diaper blowout. At that point, anything *other* than the Home Party is pretty excessive. But things change once your kid passes that first birthday. The Home Party suddenly goes from the best bet to the worst idea *ever*.

Despite having all the comforts of home, parties in your own abode are a boatload of work. Being the hostess, you'll need to clean the house from top to bottom in order to entertain. Toilets need to be sanitized and windows need to be washed and beds need to be made, just on the off chance that someone should want to see the bedrooms. And then, a few short hours later, you need to clean up all over again after your house has been destroyed by an army of wild children. Cake is ground into the couch. Tiny muddy footprints litter the floor and fingerprints adorn every surface.

More than just the mess, there's a danger in having other kids in your house. Unless parents are diligent (which they rarely are) about keeping a watchful eye on their offspring, disaster is sure to ensue. The pint-size party guests will inevitably break something or spill something or discover some secret item and display it for the entire party to see. (I won't name names, but I may just have a friend whose party was brought to a screeching halt when a two-year-old guest discovered a hot-pink vibrator and proceeded to walk out of the bedroom teething on it. Word to the wise: Lock your goodie drawer.) Plus, they're never really economical. For summer birthdays, the backyard works perfectly and entertainment can be water balloons and outdoor scavenger hunts. Winter birthdays call for entertainment and that entertainment always comes with a hefty price tag.

So, back to Ben's fifth birthday . . .

Though I wasn't too thrilled with his chosen superhero theme, I wanted to make my precious boy happy. He wanted a hero party and I was going to give him the best damn superhero party in the world. At home, of course.

I searched for days and finally found a character company not far from my neighborhood that had a Spider-Man option. Spidey would come to the house and direct a "Superhero Training Workshop." I was told to buy badges and trophies as prizes, and the afternoon was planned to a T. And with the adorable red and blue cupcakes I decorated and the fantastic cape-making project I assembled, it would be the party to put all other parties to shame. It would be the talk of the town. It would be epic.

Unfortunately, it was epic for all the wrong reasons. The

punk from the party company arrived forty-five minutes late. When he finally waltzed through the door to a room of restless little boys, he seemed blissfully unaware of the carefully orchestrated "training program" I had planned with his boss. Instead of "training" the kids, he spent the next half hour running away from them as they shouted, "You're not the real Spider-Man!" and tried to rip off his costume. Ben watched helplessly. The clueless eighteen-year-old attempted to play Simon Says with the kids, but they weren't having it. Finally, he tried to impress the crowd by climbing a tree in our yard. He climbed to the top branch and succeeded in wowing the crowd. That is, until the tree started swaying and everyone grabbed his or her child and darted away from the scene. Nothing like a tree falling on the crowd to put the kibosh on a dying party. As I escorted Spidey to the door, Jeff shot me a look that clearly said, "Bounce Zone would have been *such* a better party." Worst of all, he was right.

The hours I spent planning and creating and outdoing were wasted and I had nothing to show for it. Ben had a fine time, but would have been just as happy at the party he requested. Admittedly, he probably would have had a *better* time. Once everyone left, I sat at the kitchen table in tears. It was his party and I'd cry if I wanted to.

But that wasn't my worst party-throwing adventure. I'd have to say that Evan's third birthday takes the cake. I figured that as the third child, he didn't really *need* a party. We'd do a few presents and spend the day together and have cake as a family. It would be *fine*. He was three . . . he'd never know the difference. But, to my great surprise, my baby woke up on December 7 in the very best of moods. "It's my birthday," he happily exclaimed. "My party is today!"

It was like I'd been stabbed in the heart. The mommy guilt was unbearable.

Like any guilt-ridden mother would, I spent the day running around like a lunatic getting all the makings for an impromptu birthday party. Balloons, check. Party plates, napkins, and cups, check. Cupcakes and three candles, check. Pizza and ice cream, check. Party hats, check. Available friends with young children, check.

I accomplished a pretty impressive amount during the five hours he was at school, if I do say so myself. I picked the birthday boy up and excitedly brought him home to see the setup. Good job, Mommy! Way to turn it around!

We ate pizza and sang "Happy Birthday" and took pictures and I put the kids in their pajamas. What a day. Just as I was patting myself on the back, and pouring a glass of much-needed wine, I heard a key in the front door. My heart dropped. It was a key belonging to my husband. A husband with whom I had discussed a quiet birthday night at home. A husband who left work early to be there on time for cake. A husband whom, until that moment, I had completely forgotten about.

"Where's the birthday boy?" he greeted us. "Everyone ready for some cake?"

Whoops. I *knew* I had forgotten something.

Like I said, there is a reason everyone has parties at those indoor gyms.

Damn geniuses.

Chapter 19

SEARCHING
FOR MARY POPPINS

Mommy Confessions

• I choose ugly babysitters because I don't want my kids thinking anyone is prettier than me.

• I fired my nanny because my son was starting to favor her over me and I couldn't handle it. I told everyone that she quit.

• Nobody is good enough or responsible enough to watch my children. I'd rather never leave them than risk something happening because I needed space.

• I found private text messages to our babysitter on my husband's phone . . . I'm devastated. So glad I could pay ten dollars an hour to facilitate their romance.

• My husband travels once a week for work. Every week, for the past four years, I've gotten a sitter and gone out to dinner and a movie alone. It's the highlight of my week.

• The only people I feel safe about babysitting my kids are blood relatives. I can't believe the way some of my friends leave their kids with complete strangers.

• I never called my sitter's references.

• I make my kids nap on days when a babysitter is coming that night. No way am I paying her fifteen bucks an hour to deal with sleeping kids.

• My mother is the worst babysitter on earth.

• My kids' babysitter just called to let me know my son slammed his head on the floor, but that she would let me know if he seems to have a concussion . . . ummm, I think it's time to go home now.

• I have no friends . . . considering hiring my kids' babysitter to hang out with me.

• I stalk my babysitter on Facebook obsessively.

There is an unspoken rule of motherhood that if you come across a fellow mother in need, you offer to help her if you can. You hold the door for the mom struggling with the screaming toddler and the giant infant carrier, you offer a wipe to the mom rummaging through her bag when faced with a dirt-covered preschooler, and you pull out a snack if it could possibly fend off a meltdown for a mom who seems at the end of her rope. Once you've been in all those positions yourself, it's really second nature. Plus, it's just the right thing to do.

There's one thing, however, that you're *not* expected to offer a hand with. If you are lucky enough to score a good one, you do everything in your power to protect your find. When a mother moans about having nobody to watch the kids for her standing Saturday night date, you busy yourself with e-mail or pretend to hear a thud on the playground. You sympathize with the mom who needs help when she goes to Vegas with her girlfriends, but don't dream of sharing the first phone number on your speed dial. No way in hell are you giving up that name. You worked your ass off for it and are simply protecting your investment. It's simply instinctive.

I'm talking about the babysitter, of course, who is to be guarded with dear life.

Finding a good babysitter is one of the hardest tasks any mother faces. The sitter should be someone who is trustworthy enough to be left with your most precious possessions and still fun enough that the kids are *willing* to be left with her. A perfect babysitter will be capable of entertaining them *and* cleaning up after them. Be a playmate *and* a disciplinarian. Be great company but still available on Saturday nights. It's an almost impossible feat.

Miraculously, I have managed to find some amazing sitters for my kids. A few have been neighbors, and one I actually discovered in an online ad. They are sitters who bring over art projects and toys they no longer play with and voluntarily drop by birthday parties and dance recitals. They are unfazed by the rowdiness at my house and shuffle us out the door with a "No problem." They leave the house cleaner than they found it and are worth every penny they are paid. They are my saving grace.

Of course, we've had our share of less than desirable sitters, too. There was the one who forgot to pick up four-year-old Lily at the bus stop not once, but twice, because *General Hospital* was just *that* riveting to her. Another sitter spent her time playing on the Internet, leaving evidence of a less-than-innocent existence for us to find on the computer upon returning home. Yet another one left the freshly cleaned house a complete disaster zone, forgot to walk the dog, and allowed the kids to stay up watching TV until midnight. And then there was the one who seemed perfect online, with glowing references and rave reviews, who fled my house after meeting my kids and was never heard from again.

There is one upside to the bad babysitters, though: they make me feel better about my own parenting skills. When Lily used to take the bus, *I* never once forgot her at the bus stop. *I* always manage to have the kids asleep by *at least* 11:00 p.m. and (usually) even remember to walk the dog. Much as I want to run away sometimes, like that sitter who never came back, *I* always manage to come home to my children and parent them in a pretty decent way. The bad sitters make me feel like my kids could have done a lot worse than me.

Unfortunately, the good sitters have the exact opposite effect. One of our good ones always has the kids asleep by the time we come home at 8:30 p.m., a rare occurrence when I'm in charge. Another actually got them to eat broccoli, which is nothing short of a miracle, and last year, our summer babysitter volunteered to take the kids to downtown DC for the day, despite my recommendation that she rethink the plans. Tackling downtown DC with my kids isn't something I'd wish on anyone and something I avoid at all costs myself, but she was adamant. They took the subway and walked on the National Mall and visited museums, and

I heard they were complete angels the entire time. They never, ever would have been angelic for me. It's *those* sitters who leave me questioning my own parenting skills. I swear, at fifteen they are better at parenting than I am. It's downright embarrassing.

Sadly, it's the least of the ways I've embarrassed myself in front of babysitters in the last eight years. When we were new to our neighborhood, a young woman stopped by one night to welcome us to the hood. She brought over her phone number in case we ever needed anything and complimented me on the kids, who were getting ready to take a bath. "Thank you," I said, trying to keep our dog away from her dog and a naked Evan from running into the street. "Do you have kids of your own?" I asked, trying to make polite conversation. "Um, no?" she stammered. "I'm only . . . fourteen." As if my hole wasn't deep enough, I proceeded to inform her that theoretically, she *could* have children if she got started early, but that I wouldn't recommend it. And then I gave her a modified version of the sex talk. Remarkably, she's become one of our favorite sitters. And in the daylight, she doesn't look a day over sixteen.

Back in the days when I babysat every Saturday night—what else was a frizzy-haired girl with bad skin and no boobs supposed to do?—I spent my time rifling through bedroom drawers and devouring pints of ice cream in between calls to friends. Sure, I kept the kids alive, but just barely. Frankly, they just weren't my priority. What was my priority? Fantasizing about the father of the kids for whom I babysat. He was *dreamy*. So what if he had a slight porn habit? He was going to take me to my prom and, one day after college, we would be married. He just didn't know it yet.

I cringe when I think about that old saying "What goes around comes around." Perhaps my sitters have gone digging in my bedside drawer and made a battery-operated discovery. Or three. I wouldn't be surprised if I turned over the cushions on my couch and found old pizza slices and orange soda stains. And it would serve me right to learn that my sitter made long-distance calls to a boyfriend in Europe.

The sad thing is, even if I found any (or all) of this to be true, I still would guard my babysitters' phone numbers with my life. They are mine, warts and all, and I'm not sharing. There are some things worth sacrificing a bit of privacy and pizza money for, and a night out with my husband is one of them.

Chapter 20

THE XANAX APPROACH TO PARENTING

Mommy Confessions

• Soccer, ballet, painting, karate, speech therapy, swimming . . . When did I become a fucking chauffeur?

• I put my kids to bed in their clothes so I don't need to get them dressed the next day.

• I clock out of motherhood at 8:00 p.m. I'm so done that I walk out even if they aren't all tucked in bed and go hide in the basement with my laptop and a beer.

• My kids eat the same exact lunch every day because it's the easiest for me to make them.

• I have never actually played with my kids. I'll read with them, ride bikes, et cetera, but play Barbies or tea party? No thanks.

• If I took the amount of money I spend on my kids' after-school activities and actually put it toward myself, I'd be a hundred times happier.

• I spend more time in my minivan driving kids to activities than in any other single place. I hate it.

• My kids ride the school bus because I'm too lazy to drive them every morning.

• No matter how old you are, no matter how badass you think you are, if a toddler hands you his ringing toy phone, you fucking answer it.

• Is it bad that I want to have another baby just to give my son a playmate? So tired of rolling around on the floor with him.

• Sometimes, my daughter plays maid and cleans up the house. It's the best thing ever.

• I hate reading bedtime stories. I only do it because I know I have to. Sometimes, I just let them fall asleep watching TV.

• I didn't like playing with other kids when I WAS a kid. I certainly don't like it now.

• My kid never took ballet because I was too lazy to deal with practice and recitals.

There is no such thing as a perfect parent. We all (or most of us) do the very best we can, succeeding at some aspects of parenting and failing miserably at others. There isn't a day that goes by that I don't show and tell my kids just how much I love them. We roll down the windows in the car and sing at the top of our lungs, and unless there's lightning, I have no problem letting them run around joyously in the rain, splashing in puddles. We do art projects and bake together and have sweet, tender moments throughout the day when I feel like an exceptional mother.

And then there are the other moments that showcase my weaknesses. More than once, I've been horrified to think that a neighbor most likely heard just how loudly I yelled at the kids as they were walking the dog by our house. I don't change the kids' sheets often enough and I've been known to accidentally make them bleed while cutting their nails. But perhaps my biggest parenting flaw of all is my laziness.

For the last several years, the kids haven't been ready for bed anywhere near seven o'clock, but I am *more* than ready to be finished with them by then. The day has been long, the night has been longer, and I am done. Stick a fork in me, done. Unfortunately, my charming children are not. All three are night owls and not ready to call it a day until well past nine most nights. The solution? They need to entertain themselves. I want *nothing* to do with them.

Every night, after dinner and their baths, the kids retreat upstairs to play together and remain up there, alone, for hours. They know I'm not going to entertain them and it's either sleep or play, and they always choose play. Hours of playing house and grocery store and airport and vacation and vet before they are tired enough for bed. Hours of making forts and lining up their animals as patients and arranging dolls as restaurant patrons. They play and play and play endlessly while I get to watch TV, talk with my husband, or work on the computer. *Ignore them.*

The silver lining in all this is that my kids, unlike so many I know, are content just being left alone to explore by themselves. Imaginary play requires nothing from us, the parents, and it's *almost* like having them asleep for the night at seven thirty. Or close. For them, it's really fostered their sibling relationship and they do consider one another their best friends.

This relaxed sleep routine goes back to when they were infants. I simply hated to hear the kids cry, especially when they were so easily comforted by nothing other than my touch, so we often slept together. They all napped on the couch, cuddled up to me as I wrote, or fell asleep in the car if we were out running errands. It was just so much easier than having to bring them upstairs, rock them to sleep, and deal with their incessant crying.

There was no strict bedtime, either. When they seemed tired, we'd put them to bed, but it wasn't solely because the clock struck seven. Now, I'm not endorsing my way of doing things—I do think there is something to be said for getting kids into a tight routine. I'm completely envious of my friends whose children are all asleep by seven thirty and who know, with absolute certainty, that they will be the next night as well. But my way isn't completely without benefits. The upside of *not* maintaining a routine is more flexible children. Mine don't get bent out of shape sleeping on vacation or dealing with circumstances outside of the ordinary. They sleep when they're tired, on their own time. It works for us.

Back when Lily was a newborn, I would make all of the day's bottles in bulk, lining them up in neat little rows on the top shelf of the fridge first thing in the morning. I figured as long as I couldn't have the convenience and ease of simply whipping out a boob, I may as well make things as easy for myself as humanly possible. Sensible, right? I certainly thought so.

It never even dawned on me to heat those premade bottles, until my mother-in-law noted that I was feeding my precious warm-blooded little angel ice-cold milk. "That can't be comfortable in the middle of winter," she volunteered. "*I* wouldn't want to drink freezing milk at three in the morning!" Much as I didn't appreciate the unsolicited input, I had to admit it wasn't an *entirely* off-base observation. They *were* pretty cold and it *was* the middle of winter. But Lily took them just fine and my pediatrician said it didn't matter if they were warmed up or not. Why make her picky about something when she didn't know the difference, anyway? She was eating and gaining weight and I wasn't going to change a thing. So there.

Looking back at those early days, I remember that her face *did* seem to jolt wide awake when I fed her, and it mustn't have been all too comfortable on her little belly, but it did save me a few precious hours in the middle of the night. As far as I know, she's not still holding the cold bottles against me.

I don't think I scarred her by using cold wipes when I changed her diaper, either. The bulky wipe warmer I received as a shower gift was promptly exchanged for diapers, which I simply couldn't keep well stocked. Of all the unnecessary parenting steps, wipe warmers may indeed take the cake. I never understood why a mother would possibly want her child to get used to a nice toasty wipe-down—what happens when you're out at the grocery store or in the car or on an airplane? Wipes can't always be brought to a dreamy eighty degrees if you ever plan on leaving the house. Better to just get the baby accustomed to the chilly wipe right from the start. Plus, the less comfortable it is, perhaps the more willing she will be to get potty trained in a few years.

Speaking of diapers and ease, my kids got changed anywhere and everywhere. I'm always amused by parents who schlep around fancy portable changing stations or own designer changing tables lined with terry cloth. Kind of silly, no? It *is* shit we're talking about, after all. I plopped my kids right on the kitchen floor or the ottoman or wherever was convenient and that's where we did our business. It was far easier than having to march upstairs a hundred times a day, and an old towel was just as effective as some overpriced gingham cover thing. And fancy diaper disposal systems? Pfft. I refused to buy expensive refill bags when I could just use the ones I already had from the grocery store. It would be like flushing the toilet with Perrier.

I have a friend. Well, sort of a friend, depending on your exact definition of the word. This "friend" of mine is the *perfect* specimen of a mother. If you were to google the term "good mother," her picture would probably be the first one to come up. Her son is involved in every kind of sport and activity you can possibly imagine. He's an "exceptionally skilled" athlete and a gifted student as well. He is kind and generous and gives half of his hard-earned allowance to charity each week. He is like this, no doubt, thanks to the countless hours and thousands of dollars his mother spends carting him around to various specialists and experts. She gave up her own promising career and has made it her mission to give her only child every opportunity under the sun. Making plans with her takes months because her schedule is so jam-packed with the child's activities that she can barely squeeze in a coffee date. When I do run into her, she looks frazzled and exhausted and drained. Raising the perfect child takes effort and she is 110 percent committed to the job. And it seems to be paying off.

Her boy is a well-adjusted, happy kid. He proudly boasts about his latest karate belt and displays his track trophies on his long bedroom bookshelf. He speaks Spanish almost fluently and loves conversing with the housekeeper when nobody else can follow along. He is absolutely bright and confident and no doubt will excel in school. But I wonder whether he'd be just as great a kid, and she might be a happier parent, without all the extra effort?

I know many parents who are like this, to varying degrees. Their weekends are jam-packed with sports and art classes and socializing. During the week, the kids are in school all day, with extracurricular activities lined up until dinnertime. The moms spend hours in the car just shuttling kids back and forth, keeping the appropriate changes of clothes in the trunk. Activities, meant to be supplementary and enjoyable, have become just another chore. Their kids are definitely benefiting, but they're driving themselves a little crazy in the process.

I'd much rather pop a Xanax and focus on an activity or two that my children really enjoy than overwhelm myself (and them) with a dozen. Kids simply can't excel at *everything*. And that shit is expensive. The memberships and uniforms and coaches' gifts all add up and before you know it, you're broke. I remember wanting to faint when I found out the cost of Lily's first dance recital uniform, which she would be wearing exactly one time, for one hour. It was more than I'd spent on myself all month—were they kidding?!

I honestly don't think a child ever ended up in therapy because she *didn't* get to take advanced painting as an eight-year-old. No teen is crying over not having mastered every sport before school even started, and colleges could care less what your kid did before high school. Childhood is such a fleeting time and I really want my kids to just *enjoy* it. Equally as important, I want to come out on the other side still sane and somewhat in one piece. If I didn't have a couple of hours to myself at the end of the day, there is no doubt in my mind that I would be certifiably insane. I love my kids to death, but OMG, those punks can be annoying. Space from them is not only desirable but completely necessary. After all, part of parenthood is taking some time for ourselves, too.

But really, what do I know? My kids will no doubt be sitting on the couch complaining about the cold formula I fed them.

Can't win them all.

Chapter 21

THE TWELVE-FOOT-DEEP DEATH TRAP (AKA THE POOL)

Mommy Confessions

• I never take my kids to the pool because I don't want to wear a bathing suit in public.

• I'm thirty-eight years old and I still pee in the pool.

• I told my kids the pool was closed today because I'm feeling too fat to put on a bathing suit.

• Why does throwing our kids into giant vats of deep water ever sound like a good time? Who came up with this and what happened to good old-fashioned sprinklers?

• Whoever invented the blow-up pool has never met my child . . . and his determination to destroy all things inflatable.

• The pool is my single favorite place to go every summer . . . the kids jump in the pool with their dad and I wave from my lawn chair with my margarita. I don't want it to end.

• Years ago I told my husband I can't swim . . . the truth is I have very difficult hair and don't want to get it wet.

• When we drive past public pools I envision all those people frolicking in urine and having a great time . . . I will never take my kids.

• I had to jump into a pool fully clothed to help my daughter. I was glad to help her, but my white T-shirt was mortified.

• I'm thirty-two years old and I still plug my nose when I jump into a pool.

• My kids were forced to learn to swim so that I could relax by the poolside . . . now I see them swimming in the deep end and can't relax by the poolside.

• I'm not sure why ALL swimsuits aren't installed with a floatable device . . . that would make the most sense, right?

• The pool is not the best place to discover that you have your period. Especially with a highly observant two-year-old accompanying you.

One of the best things about having kids is being able to see familiar things through their new, innocent eyes. Through them, we can once again appreciate all the little things we'd long forgotten ourselves. Clouds once again transform into imaginary flying horses and hopping frog princes. Rainbows are more miraculous than ever and even grilled cheese sandwiches are more delicious than they were two decades ago. And then there are the things that *used* to be wonderful, but with kids became something else entirely. Something awful.

I'm talking about the pool. That crystal-clear body of water that used to be associated with golden tans, pure relaxation, and all things good. The tropical smell of suntan lotion wafting through the air and poolside burgers and fries. Cheesy romance novels bordering on soft-core porn along with delicious alcoholic beverages. The biggest stress at the pool: imperfect tan lines.

Until kids, I mean. With kids, everything about the pool is stressful.

The stress begins at home, long before that first step in the too-chilly water. It can begin days or even weeks before the first trip, even. The mere thought of it is enough to send me into a psychotic rage, throwing various items around my bedroom like a possessed lunatic. It's called finding a bathing suit to wear, and it's something no out-of-shape mother should be subjected to.

Now, this is not to say that I was the most comfortable swimsuit wearer before I had kids. *Hardly.* But, in retrospect, I should have been. The remnants my children have left on my body are never more visible than when I'm wearing a bathing suit, and it ain't pretty. I have cellulite in places that didn't even previously exist. Where my skin used to be smooth, it's bumpy, and I seem to look three months pregnant, despite not being knocked up even a little. This postbaby body is just not made for swimsuits.

Once I have somehow settled on the actual suit, after trying on the seven I own and vowing to invest in one of those "miracle suits" that are guaranteed to make me look three sizes smaller next time, it's time to begin the hair removal process. These days, this can take a full hour from start to finish. (I mean, seriously, when did my *toes* sprout hair?!) It's a much, much longer process than it was ever meant to be. Finally, it's time for cover-up selection and sunscreen application. Getting the kids all dressed and protected is another half hour, and then, *finally,* we're out the door. Let the fun begin!

Once we arrive at the pool, one of the first people I always spot is my archnemesis. The moment I see her, I immediately go all *Crouching Tiger, Hidden Dragon.* Images of long swords nearly missing her eyes fill my head in slow motion. I could take her down if I had to. Never mind *have* to, I want to. I want to see blood splatter in every direction and sport a black eye as proof of our battle. It's a fight I'm proud to have.

Okay, so we're not *really* enemies, since it would require her to actually know I exist.

Come to think of it, I don't even know her name. But still, I'm not a big fan of hers, and for good reason. Well, *understandable* reason, at least . . . As I huff and puff my way into the pool area, snapping at my children and dripping with sweat and tangible frustration, she glides onto the cement, effortlessly. She has a baby in her arms and three other children obediently by her side while my three fight over my two hands the whole time. She always looks like a million bucks, this horrid woman, her tanned body rocking the killer—gasp, *white*—bikini. She's composed, her hair is impeccable, and she's always laughing. The first few times I saw her, I logically presumed she was the Swedish nanny—what mother of four looks like that?! A gorgeous nanny, I could live with. It was still annoying how enjoyable she found the whole hellacious experience, but I didn't find it personally offensive. She was getting paid for it—it was her *job* to have fun! Unfortunately, though, last summer, I got the devastating news. She's their mother; all of them. Four young children, whom she carried and birthed, ranging from an infant to a five-year-old. She held them in that washboard stomach and nursed them from those perky tits. And that is why I despise her, Mrs. Fucking Swimsuit Model.

I do my very best to ignore her and concentrate on the task at hand: the water. For some reason, until I had kids, the notion of people frolicking in communal pools didn't really get to me. Maybe it's because I was always clean and naively assumed that others were as well. Once I had kids, though, I learned firsthand just how nasty the little creatures are. The way they sweat and the way their feet stink. The skinned, bloody knees and the way they eat their own boogies. They are just gross, gross creatures. Suddenly, sharing a big, warm bath with them isn't so appealing.

And that's on a *good* day. On a bad day, you'll hear children announce that they just peed in the pool, making you realize that they can't be the only ones and the pool is green for a reason. And then things can get really shitty. Everyone has been inconvenienced by some kid taking a crap in the water, but can all mothers claim that child as their very own? I can. It happened on the hottest day of the summer a few years ago, and the pool was shut down for a full twenty-four hours after Evan identified the floating brown thing as his own. Not the best way to make friends in a new neighborhood, that's for sure.

And then there's my own meshuggaas. Water happens to be the one place where I hang up my cool, relaxed mom hat and become the neurotic mother who normally drives me nuts. But water is *scary*. If the kids trip and fall running, they'll get a bruised knee. If they fall off of a swing, they might get a bump on the head. But accidents in the water? That's a whole other ball game, and not one that I want to mess around with. No way am

I going to trust a bikini-wearing, sixteen-year-old lifeguard with my most precious belongings. When I am at the pool, I take my job very seriously. My job? Keep my children alive.

I glance around and see other mothers of young children engrossed in their books or glancing up from conversation and wonder how on earth they can be so relaxed. And then I feel that I need to keep an eye on *their* children as well. I may as well buy a lifeguard shirt and get a whistle. Who thought it a good idea to put children in an environment they could drown in, anyway? For me, fun is entirely out of the question. It's about survival.

My kids, on the other hand, think it's the best thing ever. "Mommy, look at me do a flip!" "Mommy, watch me hold my breath!" "Mommy, did you see that?!" "*Mommy! Mommy! Mommy!*" I swear, I get whiplash just from following their directions.

It's fucking exhausting.

Unlike me, my kids are never, ever ready to leave the pool, no matter how long I have suffered. We swim for a few hours, have a snack, and then they want to swim some more. We play Marco Polo and I give piggyback rides. We play in the sandbox and then the pool again. It's *never* enough.

In order to actually get out of this twelve-foot-deep death trap, I'm always stuck bribing them with ice cream or threatening them with "If you don't stop acting like this, we *won't* be coming back." It's a threat that I actually mean and would love to follow through with. If I can't leave without three children melting down and making a scene, I *won't* do it again. The rare punishment that would actually benefit *me*.

Unfortunately, the threats inevitably whip them into shape, and we're back sooner rather than later. At the pool. Otherwise known as hell on earth.

Chapter 22

DIDN'T I ALREADY
GRADUATE?

Mommy Confessions

• TV taught my daughter to read and I took the credit. Thanks, PBS Kids! You're the best!

• When my daughter asked me what comes after a trillion I told her "a gazillion." Um, we are homeschoolers. Not supposed to just make shit up.

• My daughter's homework confuses me. She's nine.

• Do kids really need to learn how to spell? Isn't that what spell-check is for?

• I sincerely hope my kids get my looks and my husband's brains. If it's the other way around, they're screwed.

• If public schools are free, why in the world am I constantly writing them checks?

• I homeschool my kids. Honestly, I have no idea what the hell I am doing.

• I suspect my son will surpass me in math by about fourth grade . . . I'm tempted to tell him he actually doesn't need any more math than that to succeed in the real world.

• I do all of my daughter's school projects for her. It's nice to actually DO something for a change.

• I refuse to sign up for PTA. Been there, done that. Wish I could go back and warn the sweet, naive young me who once tried to "get involved"!

• God bless recess teachers . . . walking around a playground filled with hundreds of children is something I actually have nightmares about.

• I wonder whether my kids' teachers are as excited about summer starting as I am about school starting back up.

• My daughter is learning about topic sentences, supporting details, and conclusions. Huh? Better her than me.

• I can't stand kids. Too bad I'm an elementary school teacher.

• I pack healthy lunches for my kids solely because I don't want their teachers to judge me.

• I yelled at my son all morning for being difficult and slow . . . the school just called for me to pick him up; he's got a 103 fever. I feel like an ass.

- I'm terrified that my son will be a nerd and get bullied like I was. I don't want that kind of pain for him.

- I wish I was one of those moms who miss their kids when they're at school, but some school days are just not long enough.

- I've never, ever volunteered at my kid's school and I'm a stay-at-home mom.

- I let my kids stay home sick from school when I know they're not even sick because I like the company.

- Most nights, I end up doing my son's homework for him. It's wrong, but just so much easier.

- My four-year-old is going to think I'm an idiot because I keep answering his 32,094,230,940 questions with "I don't know" or "Ask Daddy."

A few years ago, my dad sold the town house he'd been living in since I was a college student. When it came time to move from the place, he presented me with a big box containing all of my transcripts and report cards from kindergarten through senior year of college. Some of the papers I'd never even seen and some I had long ago tried to banish from my memory. As I thumbed through them all, I was struck with a single thought: my children sure as hell better be more impressive students than I was.

My grades weren't *awful,* not bad even, but phrases like "lack of focus" and "not living up to potential" were echoed year after year after year. Teachers criticized my inability to concentrate on the task at hand, claiming I was a daydreamer and a doodler. They said I lacked ambition. It was clear that I just "wasn't giving it my all." But I couldn't help it. I didn't *like* sitting in a classroom when the weather was a balmy seventy-five, and the grass was a far more comfortable location to learn. I didn't *like* taking tests or worrying about grades or rehearsing for speeches on states I'd never been to. I resented being told that I held my pencil the wrong way or, later, that typing one-handed was incorrect. When I graduated, I swear, I heard the angels singing from the heavens. (Or perhaps it was my teachers. Either way.) Halle*freaking*lujah. I was done!

Or so I thought.

The feeling hit me as I was walking down the halls during Lily's kindergarten orientation, like a ton of heavy textbooks. The little desks and lockers and chalkboards filled me with familiar dread. The building even smelled like the exact same mix of industrial cleaning supplies and musty old library books that I remember my own school having, twenty years before.

I was back. And there was *nothing* I could do about it.

Ben is in kindergarten this year and it serves as a constant reminder that I have yet to master even the most basic of skills. Penmanship, for instance. I'd argue that his handwriting is more legible than mine at this point. These days, I can barely read my own notes. I would have made a really good doctor, at least where handwriting is concerned. The other big lesson he's studying? Sharing—a skill I've never quite mastered myself. If I could password-protect everything belonging to me, I would. My food, my computer, my bed—they're all mine! Hell, I would draw a permanent line down the middle of our king-size bed to prevent interlocking legs or wandering arms belonging to my sleeping husband. I frequently wake him with "That's my side!" when he's coming dangerously close to invading my personal space. I don't share drinks with the kids because of that backwash thing, and I resent giving up the last bite of my dessert. What's mine is mine and what's theirs is theirs. Clearly, I wasn't paying attention in school even at the age of five.

And then there's the homework. As a student, it just seemed horribly unfair to have to continue the fractions and spelling when I was done with the day, when Barbie dolls and crayons called my name. I stomped my feet and fought with my parents and did everything I could do to get out of actually sitting down and attacking the bastard. It sucked to be me. As a parent, it sucks more.

Though Lily is only eight, her homework assignments perplex me. All those years of falling asleep in math class and having successfully convinced my principal to let me drop calculus for pottery have come back to haunt me. Even her English work is over my head. Sure, I know how to properly write a sentence, but dissect it? No clue. Predicates? Clauses? Compound sentences? I'm already drowning. Years and years of confusion and frustration at the kitchen table have flashed before my eyes. Screaming matches, hair pulling, and tears, from both of us. If this is lower elementary, how the hell am I going to survive the later grades? Turns out, I'm *not* smarter than a second grader.

As a parent, there's so much more to school than just school. The PTA, for example. The Parent-Teacher Association should be a thing of good. A thing of purity. A thing of grace. Unfortunately, for me, it's more like a thing that nightmares are made of, far worse than forgetting about a test or walking down the halls naked.

I discovered, early on, that there is little room for casual volunteering at school. Once you start with, say, the gateway Halloween party or something, there is no going back—you've claimed that task for life. And it's not the actual volunteering that's bad. It's *nice* to be involved in your child's education. It's wonderful to get to know the teachers and the syllabus and to be able to envision your child in each of his or her classes. Of course. It's the other parents that kill me. Everything just has to be so . . . complicated. I was once on a party committee that took the group three hours to name. There were votes and discussions and pros and cons about a freaking *party*. Don't even get me started on how long the invitations took to settle. Days. Seriously. Just give me a task and let me do it the way I want to. *That's* the kind of volunteering I can handle.

If the PTA is overly complicated, it's usually thanks in no small part to the PTA president. No matter what the school, the state, or the religious affiliation, the PTA president is usually the same. It must be part of the job requirement. Her hair, whatever color it may be, is usually pulled back into a tight ponytail. She carries around a clipboard, and sometimes a microphone, too. She is usually dressed in some sort of high-end athletic gear, her tight ass bouncing as she quickly bolts by. She knows everything about everyone and makes coffee on par with the best shop in town. She's always in a hurry, off to extinguish (or ignite) some school fires concerning bake sales or teachers' gifts. Sure, she might look all kind and innocent, but beware: she's got motives. And those motives? To suck you into her world.

A big part of her world is the dreaded fund-raising. As a kid, it's mildly fun to go carting cookies from house to house, competing with your friends for top sales. But to a parent, fund-raising is a dirty little word. It brings out the worst in people, despite the fact that it's all for a good cause. When I was a kid, fund-raisers were limited to yearly chocolate pawning and the annual car wash. These days, it's everything from wrapping paper to calendars to soap, numerous times throughout the year. Parents camp out at grocery stores and movie theaters and peddle the goods at office lunches and conferences. It's insanity. And who wants an overpriced roll of wrapping paper, anyway? How about something we actually *want* to buy? Alcohol, for instance. That would be the perfect school fund-raiser. Or how about a sickroom for children with lingering fevers to spend the day hanging out in instead of being at home? Or classes over winter break? Practical things that I, for one, would gladly pay for.

Even the things that once seemed the most simple for students are challenging this time around, like actually *getting* to school. For a kid, mornings might not be pleasant, but they certainly aren't all that complicated. You pretty much roll out of bed, get dressed, and get driven to school, oblivious to the behind-the-scenes action that is surely taking place. For a mother, mornings of young, school-age children are a carefully orchestrated combination of timing, skill, and luck. It's nothing short of an act of God to get three children to school by eight, looking halfway presentable.

They need to be awoken prematurely and dressed. Lunches need to be assembled. Forms need to be signed. Breakfast needs to be prepared. Teeth need to be brushed. Bags need to be packed. Shoes double laced. All before the children would even like to be awake. Or at least fully functioning. On a good day, I get everyone out the door relatively unscathed. On the challenging days? I'm dripping with sweat and hyperventilating in the car pool lane. Really, it's all almost enough to make me consider keeping the kids home day after day after day after day and just teaching them myself.

Oh, who am I kidding? I'd rather just complain.

I must have been paying attention the day they taught *that* lesson.

Chapter 23

GIRL,
REPEATED

Mommy Confessions

• I'm torn between wanting the absolute best for my daughter and being jealous that she has it so much better than I ever did.

• Being the mother of daughters, I know why some animals eat their young.

• My daughter told me today that she never wants to speak to me again. She's three. Why did I want girls, again?

• For years, I prayed for a girl. And then I had one and prayed that she'd become more like my son.

• My daughter is so much prettier than I ever was. I can't help but be jealous.

• I buy my girls nice clothes and shoes in an effort to ensure they are cool.

• If I can't survive my daughter as a toddler, how the hell am I going to get through the teenage years?

• All my life, I wanted a girl. Finally I got one and she's the biggest tomboy in the world. I love her, but kind of feel gypped.

• I don't like my daughter's teacher because she's prettier than me.

• Having a girl is so much more complicated than having boys. Not sure I'm up for this.

• I'm disappointed that my daughter is not as pretty as I imagined her.

• My daughter only whines when I'm around. Makes me think there's something suspicious in her DNA.

• I'm insanely jealous of my daughter's legs.

• My girls are the cool kids that I never was. I'm equally envious and proud.

The summer of my seventh-grade year, many of the girls in my class got their periods. Of course, we didn't call it a period back then; it was simply referred to as "it." "Did you hear so-and-so got *it* on the playground?" or "She has *it,* that's why she didn't feel like going to the party" or "When you get *it,* did you know that you need to stay in bed with the lights out all day?" All we did was think about it, whisper about it, and plan for . . . it.

The girls who were on the early end of the development chart were the lucky ones that summer. Suddenly they were experienced and so much more worldly than those of us who rushed to the bathroom, every day, to see whether we had a surprise waiting in our days-of-the-week underpants. I wasted countless hours just willing my period to arrive, waiting for the day when I would *finally* become a woman.

It came, without much pomp and circumstance, one October day of my eighth-grade year. And it was, without a doubt, the biggest disappointment of my short life. Where was the glamour? The feeling of being a grown-up? The excitement? There ought to have been a T-shirt blazoned with "I got my period and all I got was this lousy maxi pad." What a bust. Along with bidding adieu to childhood, I also said good-bye to ever confidently wearing cream pants, feeling entirely comfortable in white sheets, and not breaking out like clockwork the third week of every month. If this was the dive into womanhood that I'd been waiting for, I wished I'd appreciated childhood more. And, although it all started with a period, it was only the beginning.

Obviously, I have no experience being a boy, but I can say from personal experience that being a girl isn't easy. It's confusing and emotional and turbulent and just plain hard. Surviving it myself was no small feat, and then I was lucky enough to have a daughter. I'm starting to realize that it may even be harder the second time around.

I have the same amount of love for all my children. It's perfect and equal and if my heart were a diagram, it would be sliced up in three pieces, each individually beating for the three of them. But that love is very different when it comes to Lily versus the boys. With the boys, my love is easy and simple. They are mysterious little creatures to me—the way they run around smashing their behinds together and can shoot a Nerf gun with perfect aim, yet are unable to direct their urine into a receptacle with more than enough room. Their needs are relatively easily met and there are few layers of emotional complexity. They are foreign and bizarre and I don't see all that much of myself in them. I adore them in the purest of ways, without any other emotions junking it up.

My relationship with Lily is another story entirely. My deep love for her is combined with a mixture of awe, concern, regret, and hope. Identifying with her the way I do, I somehow have a more complicated love for her. She loves fiercely and yells loudly and feels everything so strongly. The intensity is sometimes entertaining, but more often terrifying. The scariest thing? I remember exactly how it feels.

I remember friendships being so volatile that I would scribble out girls' names in my diary only to rewrite them on new, clean paper to paste over the scribbles. I remember cutting faces out of photographs and then needing to get reprints made once we resolved that particular battle and I again wanted their images adorning my walls. I remember being told that "hate" was way too strong a word to describe someone with whom I'd just had a sleepover the week before, but I also remember knowing that hatred was *exactly* what I was feeling. I'm always taken aback by the intensity of Lily's friendships, but I shouldn't be, because I lived them, too.

I see Lily slyly eating chocolate and remember doing the exact same thing myself, as an early introduction to the world of fucked-up body image and food issues. Will she spend years yo-yoing and worrying about the fact that her body is flat in all the wrong places and round where she wishes it weren't? Is it even possible to raise a daughter who won't at some point have these issues? As painfully hard as I try, I fear that I am failing miserably.

Am I sending the wrong message by putting lipstick on before leaving the house? Should I stop getting pedicures and just embrace the au naturel way my nails were born to look? Is adding blond highlights to my mousy-brown hair telling her that her hair is any less beautiful? I wonder about it all.

I remember the person I was in high school, always on the outside looking in, and hope that she finds her place on the inside, where it's far easier, while still maintaining a strong sense of who she is. But is that an impossibility, just like looking at food simply as fuel and moving because it's natural to do so?

I want for her everything that I wanted for myself back then and never got—the date to homecoming and the close group of fun girlfriends and the popularity and the confidence and the acceptance. But as a parent, I'd kind of rather she be stuck babysitting on a Saturday night like me, where I know she is safe and sound and out of trouble.

I worry endlessly about her preteen and teen years. If this level of emotion and drama is what we're dealing with at eight, what the hell do those years have in store for us? I kid myself into thinking that we may be dealing with the worst of it now, but I know that's not the case. I dread acne and pudgy boobs and locker rooms and school dances. I ache for the time when someone breaks her heart and makes her question just how wonderful she really is. The thought that some punk could in an instant undo all of the confidence and self-assurance we have given her makes me ill.

They say you only get what you can handle, and I'm pretty sure that's why I ended up with only one girl. But I am forever thankful that the powers that be thought I was up to the task, because I wouldn't trade my girl for the world.

Even for one with less hysterics and door slamming.

Chapter 24

THE ACHING-OVARY EPIDEMIC

Mommy Confessions

• I want a baby just so I can do a dramatic announcement on my blog. Seriously.

• I like my children best when they are newborns. I like them less every year after that.

• I am dying for another baby and my husband has put his foot down. I'm devastated and tempted to "forget" to take my pills.

• The only time my husband and I have sex is when we're trying to get pregnant. I can't wait for those two lines already.

• I would be happy having a baby every year so I could always have a newborn. I'm destined to be some crazy freak with nineteen children, but I don't care.

• I used to think "baby fever" was an actual illness.

- I want to have a baby just to beat my best friend to it. She always does everything first and it pisses me off.

- I want another baby so badly that when I see puppies and kittens I automatically envision a newborn baby. I have three young kids already and DH would probably pass out if I told him I want another.

- I love having babies. Kids, I'm not so crazy about.

- I desperately want to have a baby, but only because my sister's pregnant and it kills me to see her getting so much attention.

- Sometimes I wish my son was still little—then I go to the store and hear kids screaming and I'm happy that I don't have a little one anymore.

- I told my husband I thought I wanted a baby and he came home with a freaking puppy. So not what I meant.

I absolutely, positively do not want a baby.

Three is, without a doubt, the perfect number of children for me. It's neither too few for a rowdy game of tag, nor too many to fit comfortably around the kitchen table. I love the way they look, all lined up together, separated by two years and one foot, almost exactly. I love the triangle they form when they stand in a circle and the fact that, most times, there is at least one who is not driving me totally crazy. We can still drive home a friend or two from school, but the kids have enough entertainment at home to stay busy. A family of five is just right for us.

I can't even imagine what carrying and delivering another

child would do to me; the souvenirs they have left on my body frustrate me daily. My midsection looks like a crime scene, purple spiders crawl up my legs, and my once bouncy and predictable hair is an undecided mess between curly and wavy. I have a patch of gray hair above my right temple that I attribute solely to Evan, and my hips never went back to their prebaby location. My feet are a full size larger than before and not a single one of my old high-heeled shoes even comes close to fitting my bloated, ugly-stepsister feet. I don't even want to *think* about what my vagina would look like after pushing another kid out. Let's not even go there.

For the first time in eight years, I don't have a child in diapers and that fact brings me immense joy, never mind immense savings. I no longer carry around a diaper bag, and if I'm *really* living on the edge, I can actually get away with just carrying a clutch during short outings. It's liberating. I finally got rid of all our sippy cups and crib sheets and don't miss schlepping around an infant carrier in the least. Things are finally getting easy.

I remember back when I *had* babies, looking at the mothers who were long out of the young years and feeling pity for them. How sad that they no longer had adorable little feet to tickle and baby fat to grab, I thought. Their kids were more inclined to ignore them than shower them with sloppy kisses, and nobody stopped them at the mall anymore to tell them just how very irresistible their babies were. How sad that must be for them. Poor, poor mommies.

Snort.

I'm just starting to discover the benefits of having older children: The conversations with real people instead of mere animal noises and horrible baby songs. The feelings of real pride, instead of just happiness, and the ability to enjoy doing things that I actually *want* to be doing with my family. They are turning into real human beings with real beliefs and identities, and it's an amazing transformation to witness.

And then there's the beauty of the help they can offer. Instead of simply creating *more* work, older kids can actually help lessen it. Sure, Lily changes her clothes five times a day, but she also folds the laundry and puts it in drawers. They all help set the table and pick up leaves outside and can even walk the dog. Sometimes, if I'm *really* lucky, they'll even fetch me a Diet Coke and rub my back. Having older kids is almost like having servants. For free. Seriously, it's all kinds of awesome.

Much as I do love the baby phase, I haven't forgotten just how draining and consuming and frustrating it all is. I know I'm just not up for it all again.

Really, I'm done.

So why is it that when I spot a baby out and about I get the urge to just grab it and run for dear life? The ache in my ovaries is palpable.

When friends show off newborn pictures on Facebook, I immediately go shopping for them, lusting after little pink and blue layettes and booties of my very own. I imagine Lily with the little sister she dreams of, or the boys with one more male in the house to roughhouse with. Halloween-themed costumes for four and a sweet little body falling asleep on my chest. Once again.

If I'm *really* in the zone, I fantasize about how I would announce the big news to my husband, my parents, and even my blog readers. Matching big sister and big brother T-shirts? A dinner of little Cornish hens and baby carrots? I never did do a big, dramatic reveal with my other kids, since I was so busy dry heaving and sobbing, so this could be my chance.

I waffle between wanting to rip out my IUD with my bare hands and take the plunge and wondering whether this is all just part of being a woman. Would I always feel like this, even if I ended up with six or seven children of my own? Does the baby lust ever go away, or is it just part of my DNA, programmed into me like pale skin and thin fingernails? I can never have enough candy corn, for instance, but always end up regretful and more than slightly nauseous. Would a baby have the same effect on me? I'm pretty sure it would.

And really, it doesn't matter. We can't afford it, can't agree on it, and I'm just not willing to make the necessary sacrifices. The end.

I'm most *definitely* done.

(I think.)

Chapter 25

THE MOMMY RACES

Mommy Confessions

• I think I'm a better mom than every single one of my girlfriends.

• My sister refuses to buy organic food for her family and it makes me crazy. She can afford the best—why not give it to them?

• People stare when I breast-feed my three-year-old, but we love it. I have no plans of stopping.

• I judge people who don't cloth diaper. Is your convenience worth more than the future of our planet?

• My neighbor breast-feeds her four-year-old. It makes me want to puke.

• I hate to judge other mothers, but I do. A lot.

• I think moms who formula feed are selfish. I also think that most moms give up on breast-feeding too easily—you want the best for your kids? Then give them the only normal food there is.

• The woman ahead of me at the market had a cart full of crap. No wonder her kids were fat and unruly.

• Mother dropping her kid for sleepover at my house: "No food dye, no dairy, just soy milk, only organic food, and we don't eat ANY fast food." I let them eat all the junk they wanted. They seemed fine.

• I would never want to be a stay-at-home in a million years. I would die of boredom. How do those women do it?

• I would never tell my best friend that we co-sleep. She would totally judge me.

• I'm a much better mom when other people are around to watch me.

I order pizza for dinner so often that the shop knows my order before I start to place it. I yell too often and too loudly. My car is a complete pigsty. I often forget about homework and class projects. I can't bake a proper pie to save my life. I don't love reading to my kids. I scowl at mean kids at the park. I often forget to brush their teeth. I leave the house in slippers. I don't volunteer at school enough. I love it when the kids bite their nails so I don't have to cut them. The boys' bathroom reeks of pee . . . I could go on all day. These are *my* mommy confessions.

If there were a Mother of the Year award, I certainly wouldn't be the winner. There would be no trophies lining my built-in bookshelves and no grand award ceremony to attend. No plaque of recognition would hang on my bedroom wall, there would be no tiara to waltz around in, and I certainly wouldn't hear a speech about how flawless and perfect I am. No, I'm most definitely not Mother of the Year material. Hell, I wouldn't even be a contender.

So, it's a good thing that motherhood *isn't* a competition. But it seems not everyone got the memo.

When Ben was two years old, we had an acquaintance over for a playdate. I had a few free hours in the morning, so with the help of my pal Betty Crocker, I had whipped up a plate of brownies. As I presented the tinfoil-wrapped plate to her, you would have thought I was toting a severed head, complete with live lice, on a silver platter. She recoiled as I handed it over. "Are these organic?" she asked. "Because we rarely eat sweets, and if we do, they *must* be organic and unprocessed." I had to fight my eyes from rolling out of my head, but I bit my tongue and simply replied that they were not, and I'd grab some bananas for them instead. I then had to sit through a twenty-minute lecture on how much healthier we'd be if we adopted her way of looking at food. Suffice it to say, we never had a second playdate with them. And, also, I ate the whole tray of brownies myself.

Mothers constantly fight to one-up each other, in an effort to feel better about our own parenting. It starts as soon as those two lines appear on the pregnancy test. "You're only five months along," the competitive mom will balk. "*I* looked like you do now when I delivered my baby, *and,* the day before, I participated in a triathlon." You'll hear how she gained only twenty-five pounds, remained stretch mark–free, and quelled every pregnancy craving by drinking spinach and blueberry smoothies. Her baby was miles ahead of every baby before he'd even been born, having listened to Mozart and Bach in utero. His future circumcision and vaccinations would set him up for success, and a spot at Harvard was being held for him already.

Once the baby is born, the Baby Olympics commence. When did he or she roll over? Smile? Sit up? Sleep through the night? Crawl? Walk? Run? Of course, when and how he did all of this is clearly a reflection on you, the mother, rather than just his natural course of development.

What you put into your baby is suddenly completely open for public scrutiny. Not having breast-fed my children, I was tempted to carry a sign stating, "Breast is best but I'm using formula. You win." It never ceased to amaze me the way complete strangers thought they had any right to tell me what to do with my own baby. "You're just not trying hard enough," I heard from friends and family, when they had no idea the number of hours I spent agonizing over my lack of milk production. One even had the balls to tell me I was basically feeding my baby airplane fuel. I still can't figure out how she got there.

When the kids were old enough for solids, the sign could have been altered for organic, free-range, unprocessed foods. Sure, that stuff is best for *all* of us, but a Goldfish cracker certainly never killed anyone. Making all of my own food from scratch, however, just might kill me. McDonald's once in a while isn't going to forever clog their intestines, and a few nights of too much candy around Halloween will leave no permanent scars. So, why say anything when I give my kid a sandwich on—gasp—white bread? Yours can have his lean turkey and veggies on double whole wheat and mine can have his peanut butter and jelly. They're both fed and happy and we've done our jobs.

The decision about returning to work is another one that's always sure to ignite competition. Personally, I feel like I've hit the jackpot being able to work from home on my own schedule and still spend afternoons with my children. I tried being solely at home with the kids and was unfulfilled and depressed. Working full-time from home was an even less desirable situation, leaving me downright miserable, and the mere thought of going back to an office right now makes me want to cry. So I'm home, working on and off throughout the day and night, while taking care of the kids. It's the solution I've found that works for me, but that doesn't mean it will or should work for anyone else. The stay-at-home mom versus working mom is one of the most fiercely debated issues, each side convinced that they are choosing the right way. The thing is, there's no right way for everyone. Do what's right for you. Period.

But I do get it. Deeming someone else a bad mother *can,* indeed, make you feel like a better one yourself. It's not right, it's not productive, and it's not beneficial, but it seems to be the way we're built. Shouldn't we be secure enough in our own parenting, though, that comparing ourselves to others becomes obsolete? There are moments when I am an exceptional mother and moments when I am a complete and utter failure, all in the span of a few minutes. While I certainly would prefer to be caught only in those moments of goodness, I'll also admit to the others. I wasn't a perfect person before I had kids and I'm certainly not a perfect person now that I have them. Neither are you. (But don't worry, I won't tell.)

Last year, I was eating out alone with my kids. They were

wild and disobedient and I was wondering why on earth I ever even bother to take them out of the house, for anything, *ever*. As I was about to bury my head in my hands and cry out of pure exhaustion and desperation, a woman in her eighties passed by the table. I was expecting a lecture on how my unruly children ruined her meal, or some tips on getting them to eat anything other than french fries on their plate. Her advice, however, was far more important. "Enjoy these days," she sadly warned. "They'll be over in a heartbeat and you'll miss them for the rest for your life."

I may not have appreciated the sentiment at the moment, with my pounding headache and ketchup-stained shirt, but I know that she was right. The days may last forever, but the years pass by in a blink; the secret to survival is actually remembering to take a deep breath every now and then and enjoy ourselves along the way.

And, *that's* the only way to win the mommy race.

Chapter 26

MORE
MOMMY CONFESSIONS

• I hide things in empty tampon boxes. I know my teenage son and husband wouldn't go near one.

• I think I have the most annoying seven-year-old on the planet. Will she ever stop talking? Food literally falls out of her mouth because she can't shut up long enough to eat.

• I cheat at board games to make them end faster.

• Last night I changed all the clocks in the house to an hour and a half later and sent DS to bed. It was awesome.

• I get ridiculously excited to do our taxes every year. It's the only thing my MBA has proved useful for as a stay-at-home mom.

• I punctuate the answer to 90 percent of my kids' questions with a nice big "DUH" . . . said under my breath, of course, but I think sometimes they hear. And I am glad.

• I hate being a stay-at-home mom. I know others would kill for the chance, but I get tired of being Mommy all the damn time.

• I hide my hairbrush in my underwear drawer. If this makes no sense to you . . . then you obviously don't have a ten-year-old daughter.

• Some days I love my life. I truly love my husband and my kids. They are everything to me. But sometimes I look around my life and it doesn't feel like it is mine and I wonder what the hell I am doing here.

• Hubby got all grossed out because a little breast milk touched him. I'm devising a plan to sneak it into his food.

• I think my kid has oppositional defiance disorder. I'm about to cure it with some mommy-gone-psycho disorder. My son mouthed off to me, so he is now scrubbing the toilets. If they're going to be fresh little brats, I will make their punishment work for ME!

• Sometimes I wipe my child's face slightly hard to get him back for being a fussy, whining eater.

• You know it's bad when the baby tries to nurse a fat roll instead of a boob. My number one reason for not wanting to have a third baby is that I pee my pants pretty much every day since my second was born two years ago. At this rate my kids will soon be more potty-trained than I am.

• I like sex as much or more than the next person, but after a particularly passionate encounter, one of my first thoughts is, "Whew, this ought to carry us over for a while."

• I love my daughter and my grandkids, but I have to put limits on my time with them or I would have no life of my own at all. I raised my kids, now sometimes I'm selfish and want "me" time.

• I regret being too scared to tell anyone about my postpartum depression.

• My teenage son's curly mop is COMPLETELY out of control. I fantasize about shearing him like a sheep.

• I've been a SAHM for twelve years. I'm exhausted. I want a paycheck. I want days off. I want an office that doesn't look like a bomb went off in it. I want everything I used to have.

• I put vodka in my orange juice this morning.

• I hope my kids never catch on to the fact that I have NO IDEA what the hell I'm doing.

• I have a crush on Eugene from *Tangled*. Yes, he's a cartoon character. I've reached a new low.

• I'm terrified that my baby will love her new day care providers more than me.

• I might have to pawn some jewelry to pay for day care. Totally worth it.

• My teenage son has psoriasis. I know it's not contagious, but sometimes I don't want to sit next to him.

• I ate the rest of my kids' Easter chocolate last year while PMSing and when they asked what happened to it, I told them the dog ate it.

• When my kids need to be comforted I send them to their grandma.

• I know I'm way too old for this but . . . I'm actually really sad that I'll never be a princess.

• The best time of day for me is bedtime.

• My son has removed his diaper and is beating me with it. Think that's my wake-up call that it's time to be productive today?

• I'm so drained right now that my kids could ask for a pet rattlesnake that would sleep in my bed and I'd be like, "Fine, whatever . . ."

• I would like, for just a moment, to feel like I did when I was a careless teen.

• I keep a steady supply of M&M's in my purse to fend off temper tantrums at Target.

• My girls and I had donuts for dinner.

• Some days I count down the months until my teen daughter leaves for college. She is amazing and I love her, but she is emotionally exhausting and I can't wait until I have my life back.

• Just caught my three-year-old trying really really hard to put his own weenie in his mouth. Oh. My. Many men before you have tried and failed to live the dream, son. Many men.

• When my MIL dies, I'm going to do the biggest happy dance of my life. On her gravestone.

- I bought myself a pretty pair of lilac-colored satin pajamas with a lacy camisole top that I thought DF would find sexy. I put them on and tried to make a sexy entrance into the bedroom. He said I looked like Barney.

- I'm embarrassingly excited for the new *iCarly* episode.

- I had no idea how much of parenting is just bullshitting your way through while hoping the kids don't call your bluff. I'm full of it.

- I believe in ghosts and I'm terrified of the dark.

- I wish my friends would either (a) get divorced or (b) stop calling me for venting/mediation purposes. I am not a shrink.

- My three-year-old has a TV in his room, only hooked up to a DVD player so he can watch *Sesame Street* videos at night and so I can get a break.

- I would rather pull out my own teeth than go to PTA meetings.

- My son has a poopy diaper. I just sent him upstairs and told him to sit on DH's face. Serves my husband right for sleeping so late.

- To the little shit that punched my eleven-year-old DD for no reason and bruised her arm: You're lucky I'm old and you're faster than me. To his parents: Pray we don't run into each other any time soon.

- I constantly forget to brush my one- and two-year-old's teeth. I am not sure why it's so hard for me to remember, but it's a good thing that these teeth will fall out.

• For dinner tonight I have slaved over three bowls of the finest cereal our pantry has to offer, with the rarest of milks from the fridge to complement its exquisite flavors. Dig in, kids.

• Pretty sure as the mom I'm supposed to kill the spiders for my kids and not go screaming down the hallway WITH them.

• Finally, as a mother of five, I have come to the realization that my own mother had no clue what the hell she was doing. Neither do I.

• My kids were acting like lunatics, so I sent them to their rooms. While they were up there, I ate all their Swedish fish.

• Haven't spoken to MIL directly for months, and yet she still finds ways to work herself into my happy place . . .

• I read once that if you start acting like a crazy gorilla in the middle of your child's temper tantrum, she'll stop screaming to watch you . . . it didn't work and now I feel like an ass.

• I thank God that my kid's favorite foods are mac and cheese, ramen noodles, and cheap-ass hot dogs!

• Even though I have worked steadily since I was fifteen years old, I sometimes just want to be taken care of.

• I take the long way home to enjoy the relaxation of everyone safely buckled in their car seat and not trying to crawl up me.

• I strategically clean up the crap battery-operated toys before my husband comes home, but leave out all the puzzles and books my children and I play with during the day for my husband to see.

• I came home from a weekend away on business and my kids were wearing the same pajamas I had left them in. My daughter informed me Daddy had dubbed it "Lazy Weekend." WTF?

• I want to get pregnant again. But I'm afraid of getting a boy. I don't want a boy.

• I don't have insomnia . . . I choose to stay up and sleep less hours just so I can have a glass of wine and the remote at the same time.

• Helping DD7 study for spelling test, explaining that Christmas is spelled as such because we celebrate the birth of Jesus Christ. Then had to explain, "No, that's not a bad word. Mommy just says it when she's angry. A lot."

• There is a special place in hell for people who cut in line at school pickup lines. There are freaking signs everywhere! Get a clue!

• When we were kids, my sister showed me how spraying furniture polish in the air while they were out would make our parents comment on how nice the house looked when they got home. Turns out it works for husbands, too.

• I put twenty boxes of condoms on my baby shower registry. No one found it as funny as I did.

• I knew my daughter had lice and I sent her to school anyway because I didn't want to cancel my hair appointment.

• I throw candy wrappers behind the couch and then blame the kids when my husband finds them.

• My MIL is bringing yet another load of "treasures" to our house tomorrow. When she leaves, I'm loading up my car and going to Goodwill.

• I became an alcoholic when I became a SAHM. I can't go through one day of this boring life without the buzz.

• I think I'm ruining my children. I only hope it doesn't start to show until they move out of the house. Then I can blame someone else.

• I continue co-sleeping with my four-month-old (even though I know I am setting up bad sleep habits) just because I want to hold on to the time a little bit longer.

• I use sports tape wrapped completely around my two-year-old's diapers at nap and nighttime so he doesn't strip and piss all over the pillow, creating more laundry.

• I buy store-made muffins and pass them off as my own for bake sales.

• A tab broke on my son's diaper and instead of getting a new one, I wrapped him in packing tape. We have twins; there's no room for wastefulness.

• I give my kids all the crunchy pointy french fries from McDonald's and keep the good ones for myself.

• I miss my pre-kids stomach so much it hurts.

• I was using three types of birth control (pill, condom with spermicide, diaphragm) and I still ended up pregnant. WTF was God thinking?

• I only take my two-year-old to the pool so that I can work on my tan.

• I let my daughter stay home from school because I missed her.

• Three-and-a-half-year-old proudly announced that he pooped on the potty and wiped his own butt. When I told him he needed to wash his hands he said, "I already did. In the potty."

• When did weekends become the same as every other sucky day of the week and summers the same as every other uneventful, stressful season?

• I send homemade baked goods to the teaching staff twice a month so they'll be nice to my challenging son.

• Is a smoking-hot OB reason enough to get pregnant again? I'm leaning towards yes.

• My boyfriend and I had hot sex in the shower tonight. Loud, steamy, amazing, wonderful sex. It was all ruined, though, when we walked out of the bathroom to see my four-year-old with a little boner standing outside the door. SHIT.

• I laugh when moms struggle with the terrible twos. You think two is bad? Snort. Try the teenage years.

• I've gained more weight since my last son was born than I did during both pregnancies combined.

• Whenever my son is given a really annoying toy, I make sure that he accidentally "loses" it. Overnight. When he's sound asleep.

• I eat healthy all day and exercise . . . but then get home and raid the kids' snacks.

• At the end of the day, all I really want is simple: to be able to shit in peace and quiet.

• They make my life hectic and dirty and exhausting, but I wouldn't have it any other way. Being their mother is the best part of my life, hands down.

ACKNOWLEDGMENTS

To my husband, Jeff Smokler: Not only could I never have written this book without you, I wouldn't have wanted to. Thank you for not pouting when I ridicule you and continuing to provide me with ample material. You are my rock and I can't imagine going through life alongside anyone but you. Follow you, follow me.

To my mom, Kathy Epstein: I don't think I ever truly appreciated you until I had children of my own. Thank you for always being my biggest cheerleader, no matter what the sport. Your love and encouragement knows no limits. Everyone deserves a mother like you.

To my dad, Drew Epstein: Thank you for the best legal advice I've ever received, along with never-ending five-dollar bills and love. Sandy Jacobs: Thank you for your shared excitement and support through this crazy ride.

To my brother, Matt Epstein, and sister-in-law to be, Bari Weinstock: Please hurry up and have babies, I need some inspiration! Love you both.

Lisa Leshne: You are my Jerry Maguire—so much more than just an agent. Thank you for finding me and holding my hand and becoming a friend. You are phenomenal.

Lauren McKenna: You are the best editor a girl could ask for. Thank you for making this process so much fun and laughing in all the right places. It's been a blast.

Nichole Harvey: Thank you for keeping the Scary Mommy community alive and thriving. I could never do it without you.

Thank you so much to my message board moderators who volunteer their precious time to make the boards and confessional a kinder, gentler place. You are amazing! Carri Sweeney, Samantha Angoletta, Mikki Caplan, Kristin Mason, Tamara Seidel, Charisse Oates, and Rae Thomas. And thank you to the wonderful regulars for sparking conversation, making friends, and supporting one another. I am so very proud of what we have built together.

Rachel Horner: You are the best intern in the world. Thank you for making my life easier during the craziest of times.

Nicole Daniels: I could not have written this book without your help. You are the babysitter every mother should be lucky enough to have.

Love to my family: Lisa Chinsky, Bonnie and Dick Lechtner, Ashley Strange, Larry Lechtner, Sue Mandell, Mara Landis, Carol and Myles Berkman, and Jason Guyan for your support and enthusiasm from the very beginning. It means the world to me.

Thank you, Baltimore, for adopting me with open arms. For the first time in my life, I'm not itching to move. To Jennifer Mendelsohn and Evan Serpick: I am lucky to count you as neighbors and friends. Many thanks also to: The Port Discovery Museum, *Baltimore* magazine and the *Baltimore Sun* (especially Jill Rosen) for lovely support and coverage. To my kids' teachers: I am grateful for each and every one of you. Thank you for educating my children day after day after day after day. Better you than me.

Deep appreciation to my friends who have always supported all things Scary Mommy: Marlene Lewis, Jessica Kahn, Amy Egan, Mindy Greenberg, Yana Frankel, Jessica Fidgeon, the Feldmans, the Liptons, the Hamilton women, Anat Zirkin, and Kim Glaun.

Francesca Banducci, Kathy Alconcel, and Angie Lee: In a perfect world, you girls would be my sister-wives. Thank God for the Internet.

Thank you to Cynthia Dermody and Amy Boshnack for making a writing gig at Café Mom's The Stir a pleasure rather than a chore.

I am grateful to have reconnected with Wash U friends through the magic of social media: Nina Badzin, Rebecca Kotok, Alissa Peltzman, and Alexis Tande, thank you for your dedication!

To my wonderful online friends, who have gone above and beyond in their support, especially: Galit Breen, Dawn Finicane, Ellen Seidman, Holly Rosen Fink, Loralee Choate, Sunday Stilwell, Lara DiPaola, Jennifer Gerlock, Cara Blevins, Ann Imig, Nicole Hempeck, Erin Domareki, Heather Walsh, Michael Guill, Debbie Patrick, Jen Mitchell, Becky Leatherman Adams, Corine Ingrassia, Nicole White, Kate Hood, Tracy Morrison, Brittany Vanderlinden, Loukia Zigoumis, Pauline Karwowski, Rachel Matthews, Lori Garcia, Mary Fischer, Heather Reinhard, Deborah Cruz, Amber Page, Christy Casimiro, Laura Franklin, Marinka Romanoff, Alexandra Rosas, Britt Reints, Cynthia Wheeler, Julie Dance, Tiffany Romero, Tracey Gaughran-Perez, Rachel Voorhees, Jennifer Williams, Jessica McFadden, Dani Ackerman Liberman, Jodi Schulz, Shell Jeanette, Sarah Visbeek, and Beth Morse. I'm so lucky to have you on my side.

My sincere gratitude to the crew at Simon & Schuster: Jennifer Robinson and Natalie Ebel for their publicity and marketing expertise, and Alexandra Lewis for kindly convincing me that there is never a stupid question.

And to the army of Scary Mommies all around the world who read my blog, submit their own posts, form friendships on the message boards, and confess their secrets: This book wouldn't exist without you. Thank you, from the bottom of my heart.